Simon Gray

THE LATE
MIDDLE CLASSES

NICK HERN BOOKS
London

A Nick Hern Book

The Late Middle Classes first published in Great Britain in 1999 as a paperback original by Nick Hern Books Limited, 14 Larden Road, London W3 7ST

The Late Middle Classes copyright © 1999 by Simon Gray

Simon Gray has asserted his moral right to be identified as the author of this work

Cover image: Harriet Walter as Celia (courtesy of the Palace Theatre, Watford)

Typeset by Country Setting, Kingsdown, Kent CT14 8ES

Printed and bound in Great Britain by Athenaeum Press, Gateshead NE11 0PZ

ISBN 1 85459 433 8

A CIP catalogue record for this book is available from the British Library

For Victoria

The Late Middle Classes was first presented by the Palace Theatre, Watford, on 19 March 1999, and produced on tour by the Ambassadors Theatre Group/Turnstile Group Limited. The press night was on 23 March. The production then played at Brighton, Plymouth, Bath, Woking and Richmond. The cast was as follows:

BROWNLOW	Nicholas Woodeson
HOLLY *in his forties*	not cast at press date
HOLLY *aged twelve*	not cast at press date
CELIA	Harriet Walter
CHARLES	James Fleet
ELLIE	Angela Pleasence

Director Harold Pinter
Designer Eileen Diss
Lighting Mick Hughes
Sound Designer Dominic Muldowney

ACT ONE

Scene One

BROWNLOW*'s study/sitting room. Autumn. Early evening. The present.*

A baby grand piano, a sofa, desk, table, an armchair.

BROWNLOW, *in his seventies, is sitting in armchair, dozing, muttering.*

Doorbell rings.

BROWNLOW (*mutters in his sleep, gradually wakes up, listens*). No, I couldn't have heard it – must be a dream –

Doorbell rings again.

BROWNLOW *goes to window, peers out. Knocks on window.*

BROWNLOW. Is there anybody there? Who's there? Mrs Jameson, is that you? Mr Jameson? Surely you know not to disturb me at this hour, I'm very busy –

Doorbell rings again.

BROWNLOW. Who is it? (*Agitated. Attempts to compose himself, goes out of room.*)

Voices off, indistinct.

BROWNLOW (*off*). Yes? Can I help you?

HOLLY (*off*). I don't know if you remember me. I'm Holliday Smithers.

BROWNLOW. Smithers – Holliday Smithers – yes, yes, of course I remember you.

HOLLY. I was just passing and couldn't help wondering if you were still here.

BROWNLOW. Yes, yes, still here. Well, please come in.

HOLLY enters BROWNLOW's sitting room, followed by BROWNLOW. HOLLY is in his mid-forties. He looks around.

BROWNLOW. And, um, where have you come from?

HOLLY. Well, from Australia in fact. Melbourne.

BROWNLOW. And you're staying on the island?

HOLLY. No, I'm staying in London. But I had to come down to Portsmouth for a few days.

BROWNLOW. And so you decided to pay us a visit, after all these years.

HOLLY. Well, I had the afternoon off, couldn't resist driving over – odd that, being able to drive over, all the way by road. I still imagined having to take the ferry. I'd have preferred that on such a beautiful day. Especially when everything turned out to be so familiar. (*Looks around again.*) As it is here. Except that it's all older of course.

BROWNLOW. Yes, yes, like myself.

HOLLY. Like myself. Do you mind if I sit down?

BROWNLOW. Oh – oh, yes, of course, I'm sorry – please. Where would you like? (*Gesturing around room.*)

HOLLY (*walks over to armchair, sits down, watched by BROWNLOW*). There is a change, though. No, not a change, an absence. Yes, something's missing. Oh yes, a cat. There was always a cat called Kitty-Cat. Kitty-Cat Number 7. You explained to me that your mother always called her cats Kitty-Cat so it was always the same cat to her. When one died she'd go straight on to the next Kitty-Cat almost without noticing the pain of loss or the treachery of replacement. But you numbered them in your head. So I knew Kitty-Cat Number 7.

BROWNLOW. They were called Catty-Kit, not Kitty-Cat.

HOLLY. Oh yes, sorry. I must have let the chocolate bar get in the way. Well, what number did it get up to, Catty-Kit, before its sequence ended?

BROWNLOW. Eleven. Number eleven I had put down the day after I buried my mother.

HOLLY. Ah. The end of the line then.

BROWNLOW. It felt like the end of an era.

HOLLY. Yes, I suppose it must have done. (*Little pause.*) But have you gone on keeping the same hours?

BROWNLOW. Well, I keep the hours, yes. Yes, I do that.

HOLLY. Every morning from ten to twelve and every evening from nine, was it? until midnight.

BROWNLOW. Nine thirty until midnight. Back then. Now of course my time's my own and I start earlier. Whenever I feel like it.

HOLLY. You and your beloved talking to each other. (*Glancing towards piano.*)

BROWNLOW. Yes.

HOLLY. And what do the two of you talk about these days? Anything in particular?

BROWNLOW. A concerto. We're working on a concerto. We've been at it for a long time. A long, long time. I hope to complete it before I die.

HOLLY. Oh yes, you must. You'd want to hear it after all. You used to say that you couldn't compose the opening until you knew how the piece would close. So first close, then open, and then on into the middle which would look after itself.

BROWNLOW. Well, of course one has these theories at different times of one's life. One's creative life. Perhaps it's to do with memories. The more memories you have the more difficult it all becomes.

HOLLY. You mean the memories teem about and get in the way?

BROWNLOW. Well, no, not teem about. Not quite as lively as that. They bob up.

HOLLY. What sort of memories?

BROWNLOW. Well, just memories. Of days gone by. (*Little pause.*) You, for instance. You bob up now and then. Quite often in fact.

HOLLY. Do I?

BROWNLOW. Do I ever bob up for you?

HOLLY. Oh, yes. This afternoon when I was walking about the island. I went to see the old house, well, the family house, and one thought led to another and that led to another and then finally up you bobbed again.

BROWNLOW. Like a Jack-in-the-box.

HOLLY. No, not really like a Jack-in-the-box. The thoughts were quite logically connected, I think. Though there was a bit missing – something I tried to remember and couldn't. The music. The music that seemed to run through it all. It wouldn't come back. It won't come back.

BROWNLOW. Really? Can I offer you something? Tea? Coffee? And I do believe there's some sherry somewhere – but very, very old. From my mother's day. Quite a few bottles of it there should be in the larder, Mrs Jameson helps herself to it from time to time but – she's my cleaning woman, you know, she came long after your time – after my mother's too – in fact she's only been here about ten years, I think it must be, and her husband does the gardening. Sometimes I hear them down in the kitchen, laughing and talking, and it occurs to me that they're at the sherry, especially when they're being rather loud, may I ask a question?

HOLLY *gestures.*

There is a pause.

HOLLY (*gently*). A question. You're going to ask a question.

BROWNLOW. Are you real?

HOLLY. Yes, quite real. Well, at least I think I am. One can never be completely sure on that point, can one? (*Gets up, goes over to* BROWNLOW.) But here, feel this. (*Holds out his hand.*)

BROWNLOW *tentatively moves his hand, touches* HOLLY's *sleeve. As he withdraws his hand,* HOLLY *catches it in his.*

HOLLY. There, you see. Not just the garments but flesh and blood.

They stand, hands clasped for a second. HOLLY *removes his hand.*

BROWNLOW. Did you say yes? To the sherry, that is?

HOLLY. A glass of your mother's sherry, yes, I'd love to try it at last. Thank you.

BROWNLOW. Well, I'll see what I can find. (*Goes out.*)

HOLLY *goes over to piano, picks along keyboard as if trying to work out a tune. Shakes his head in exasperation, goes back, sits in armchair, takes out cigarette, lights it. Sits back meditatively. As he does so:*

Piano music, over, as:

Lights going down as lights coming up on SMITHERS' *sitting room.*

Scene Two

Spring. Evening. Early nineteen fifties.

SMITHERS' *sitting room.*

HOLLY, *as a child of 12, playing the piano.*

HOLLY *continues to play for a second, stops. He gets up, goes over to sofa, sits down. Takes out exercise book from satchel, extracts a loose sheet of paper, reads it very intensely, then reaches urgently into satchel, fumbles deeply, takes out magazine, begins to go through it, studying pictures, occasionally reading to himself aloud but inaudibly from sheet of paper.*

Sound of front door opening and closing.

HOLLY *scrambles to his feet, stuffs magazine and exercise book back into satchel, hurries over to piano, starts playing.*

CELIA SMITHERS, *Holly's mother, enters, dressed in tennis shorts, top, carrying tennis racquet and tennis balls.*

CELIA. She's chucked! That bloody Moira woman has actually chucked! She couldn't 'phone me before I left so I could have got somebody else, no, she just stepped out as I was cycling past, with her hand raised like a policeman – I nearly peddled straight into her and I wish I had – she honked out some nonsense about coughs and sore throats, running eyes, her cheeks were like apples, my dear, great shiny apples, by far the healthiest thing I've seen all week – oh, I could kill her! Kill, kill, kill! (*Serves viciously with imaginary ball.*)

HOLLY. It's because you keep beating her.

CELIA. Oh, don't be so silly.

HOLLY. It's true. Every time you come back from playing against her you crow about beating her six love, six love. You do the same with me so I know how she feels.

CELIA. She wouldn't be so petty. Yes, she would. Everyone on this bloody island is petty. That's why you've got to win a scholarship. To get us off it.

HOLLY. That makes complete sense. That's perfectly logical. I understand that.

CELIA. You sound just like your father. (*Banging her racquet gently on his head.*) I. Won't. Have. You. Making. Fun. Of. Your. Father.

HOLLY. I wasn't making fun of him. I just don't see why my getting a scholarship would get you off the island.

CELIA. Because if you win a scholarship to St Paul's or Westminster we won't have to pay the fees and we can all move to London where we belong. And if you don't win a scholarship you'll end up going somewhere local where you'll have to be a day boy so we can afford your fees. We've been over and over it.

HOLLY. You haven't been over and over it with me.

CELIA. No. I meant your father and I have been over and over it.

HOLLY. What's wrong with Portsmouth Grammar School? A lot of boys from around here go there – all my friends – and they say it's jolly good.

CELIA. It may be jolly good for them but it's not jolly good enough for us.

HOLLY. Well, I don't think it's fair that everything you want comes down to me getting a scholarship. I probably haven't got a chance. We don't know anybody around here who's –

CELIA. Edwin Tomkins.

HOLLY. Oh, *him.*

CELIA. 'Oh, *him*' won a full scholarship to St Paul's, as his wretched parents never stop boasting. And as you despise him so much you could surely do just as well. Now, do get on with your practice, and what about your prep, have you done that yet?

HOLLY. Almost. I've just got a bit of French left.

CELIA. Then finish your practice and on with your French. I want it done before Mr Thing-me-bob comes. You're always too tired to do any prep after your piano lessons.

HOLLY *starts playing piano.*

CELIA (*watches him*). Oh, you do remind me of someone, you know, whenever you play.

HOLLY. Do I? Who?

CELIA. One of the young chaps in the war, one of the fighter pilots. He had the same – same intensity – as if there was nothing else in the world but the music, even though everybody was singing around him.

HOLLY (*plays for a little*). What happened to him?

CELIA. He went for a Burton, poor young devil, like so many of the rest of them.

HOLLY. Oh. (*Playing on.*)

CELIA. Tell me something. Something very important.

HOLLY. Oh, Mummy, I'm trying to concentrate.

CELIA. You have to answer this. Do you love me?

HOLLY (*sighs*). Of course I love you.

CELIA. Why?

HOLLY. Oh, Mummy, you know why. Because you're my mother.

CELIA. I do wish you'd once, just once, come up with a more flattering answer. What is that piece anyway, it's been driving me mad trying to remember – Beethoven, isn't it?

HOLLY. Very nearly. It's Brownlow. Mr Brownlow.

CELIA. Golly, really, you mean he writes it too? (*Staring over HOLLY's shoulder.*)

HOLLY. Oh, yes. Thomas Ambrose Brownlow.

CELIA. Ambrose? Thomas Ambrose Brownlow? Is that hyphenated? Thomas Ambrose-Brownlow?

HOLLY. No, that's his middle name I think.

CELIA. Rather precious to use your middle name. Especially when it's Ambrose. But I suppose if your name is Brownlow, Thomas Brownlow, and you want to add a little splash, if you're a composer – what's it called? (*Reading.*) Mio – 'A Bagatelle for Mio'.

HOLLY. It's miaow. It's about their cat when it miaows.

CELIA. Doesn't sound at all like a miaow to me. Except it's soft and velvety so I suppose that's a bit like a cat. What does he do with them when he's composed them? Does he have them played by people – concerts, that sort of thing?

HOLLY. He says they're doing this on the Third Programme.

CELIA. The Third Programme, golly. Well, perhaps they'll let you play it.

HOLLY. Actually, Mummy, I don't want to do the piano any more.

CELIA. What on earth do you mean?

HOLLY. I mean I don't like it. And I'm not very good at it.

CELIA. Nonsense! Your Mr Ambrose says you're the best student he's ever had. By far and away the best on the island anyway.

HOLLY. Yes, well, he doesn't really mean it, he's just being polite.

CELIA. You need your music, you know you do. You put it down on your scholarship form that you played the piano as one of your main interests.

HOLLY. No, I didn't. I put down music. And so if I change to the violin –

CELIA. The violin! How on earth do you think your father's going to afford a violin?

HOLLY. Well, we could sell the piano –

CELIA. Sell the piano! It's your legacy from your godmother. You don't just sell off legacies and buy something else you prefer.

HOLLY. I know I'd be better at the violin, I know it.

CELIA. But you'd have to start from the beginning and you've gone so far with the piano and – well, you talk it over with him (*Gesturing to music.*) – he'll know what's best.

HOLLY. He won't want me to give up the piano. And he doesn't do the violin.

CELIA. Well, there you are. As he's the only music person on the island you'll just have to stick with what he wants.

HOLLY. It's not what he wants, it's what I want.

CELIA. It isn't what you want, it's what will get you a scholarship.

HOLLY. I'll give up the extra football training if you let me do the violin.

CELIA. Don't be silly, you're captain of the first eleven, they wouldn't dream of letting you. And quite right too.

HOLLY. Can't you ask Daddy at least and he can explain to Mr Brownlow and if I only took half my pocket money we could probably find a cheap violin in Portsmouth and somebody there who can teach me.

CELIA. And who's going to ferry you there and back every time you have a lesson? Your father, I suppose, as if he hasn't got enough on his plate – oh, I haven't got time to stand here and argue about something so completely absurd, for one thing I've the evening meal to think about, all I've got are powdered eggs, a bit of lard and almost no butter –

HOLLY *bangs his hands down on the keyboard in anger and despair.*

CELIA. Don't you dare do that! How dare you do that!

HOLLY (*after a moment*). Sorry. (*Little pause.*) Sorry, Mummy. It's just that – that I'd love to learn the violin, that's all.

CELIA. Well then, darling, if we get to London you shall, I promise you. And I'll tell your father, I promise. There. I can't say fairer than that, can I?

HOLLY *nods. He picks up satchel, makes to leave the room.*

CELIA. Where are you going?

HOLLY. To my room. To finish my French.

CELIA. You can do it down here at the table where I can keep an eye on you.

HOLLY. Why?

CELIA. Because I never know what you get up to in your room these days.

HOLLY. What do you mean?

CELIA. You're blushing.

HOLLY. I'm not blushing. You were going to go out and play tennis so it wouldn't have mattered to you then where I did my prep.

CELIA. I've had enough arguments for one afternoon. I don't want to talk about any of it. That's your father's job.

HOLLY. What do you mean?

CELIA. Nothing. It's just that some things are between fathers and sons.

HOLLY. What things?

CELIA. I told you, I don't want to talk about it. It's all perfectly normal, I expect. Not that I'd know.

HOLLY. I don't understand.

CELIA. There's nothing for you to understand, I keep telling you. Now you jolly well get on with your prep, young man –

HOLLY. You mean when I was praying and you came in? Why are you against my praying?

CELIA. Holliday, not another word. Get on with it before your Mr Thing arrives.

HOLLY *takes his books over to table, opens books, begins to work.*

CELIA *watches him, then goes over to sofa, lights a cigarette. Lies on sofa, smoking, her leg jigging irritably. Suddenly struck by an idea, she gets up, goes to telephone, dials.*

CELIA (*on telephone*). Oh, Bunty dear, it's Celia. It just struck me, lovely afternoon, a bit of a breeze, what do you say to a

game of tennis? (*Little pause.*) Well, right now really. I
mean, as soon as we've changed. We can be at the court in
ten minutes – oh, don't be so silly, dear, you're a very good
natural player, all you need is practice – and weight has
nothing to do with it, many marvellous players are as heavy
as you – what? No, no, I don't mean that at all, all I mean is
something you said the other day about being worried that
you're getting a little – a little – and what better way to get
it off? (*Pause.*) Oh, very well, dear, if you really feel I'm
inviting you to join a chain gang instead of a mild knock-up
– what? Moira? No, no, she's a bit under the weather, she
says, and anyway I don't fancy an hour with Moira, all
she'll talk about is how marvellous everything is and their
wretched holiday in Ireland with all the steaks and butter
and fresh cream. Which reminds me, my dear, have you got
any eggs from those chickens of yours, I want to give
Charles a surprise, he was saying last night how much he
yearned for an omelette, but with fresh eggs, not powdered
– oh – oh, well never mind, Bunty dear, I was going to offer
you some chocolate in exchange but I expect that the last
thing you want at the moment is chocolate so it'll have to
be dried eggs again, they'll just have to put up with it –
what? Wait? Oh, somebody at the door – somebody at the
window? Oh, tapping on the window – well, I really haven't
got anything more to – (*Stands, waiting, lights another
cigarette, taps her foot irritably.*) Who is it? Moira! Tapping
on your window! What does she want? A cup of tea! Moira
taps on your window whenever she wants a cup of tea – no,
no, thank you, dear, really what I want to be is outside, you
see. Give Moira my – my –

She hangs up.

CELIA. Really, these people – these people on this bloody
island, I don't know how I put up with them. Always
presuming on one's friendship. If they didn't claim to be
friends they wouldn't dare to do the kind of thing they do
do. Of course it's easy for them, they've both got help, they
can play tennis or have their cups of tea with each other
whenever they like. While I – what on earth was the point
of our winning the war if you end up worse off than before

it started? No housekeeper, no maid, while both of them
have got both. And Bunty's even got a gardener. Well, she
calls him a gardener but really he looks like a convict –
pasty-faced and furtive and smoking, and doesn't even
know how to say good morning. Doesn't speak at all as far
as I know. He may be one of those eye-tie prisoners of war
who stayed on. But if you've got an Italian prisoner of war
in your garden I suppose you do feel you've won the war
and everything's almost back to normal. In spite of Winnie
being thrown out.

She looks at HOLLY *who is bent over exercise book,*
writing. CELIA *sits on sofa, allows her lids to become*
slack, her eyes vacant.

HOLLY glances towards her, then slides piece of paper out
of his pocket, puts it into exercise book, begins to read.
Becomes increasingly aware of stillness from sofa.

HOLLY. Mummy? Mummy? (*Stares towards her anxiously as*
he closes exercise book, puts it into his satchel, goes across
to CELIA *with increasing terror, stares down.*) Mummy –
oh, Mummy, what is it? What is it? Oh – (*Wrings his hands,*
looks around.) Daddy, Daddy – (*Runs to telephone, dials*
frantically.)

CELIA (*looks towards* HOLLY). What are you doing? Who
are you 'phoning?

HOLLY puts down telephone, stares at her with relieved
disbelief.

CELIA. Who were you 'phoning?

HOLLY. Daddy.

CELIA. Why?

HOLLY. Because – because I thought you were dead.

CELIA. Oh, don't be such a fool. I was just lying here thinking
about things. Concentrating.

HOLLY (*realising*). No you weren't. You were pretending. You
were pretending to be dead.

CELIA. I was doing no such thing. I – I –

HOLLY. Yes you were, you were! Why were you? You're always doing things like that – why? (*On the verge of tears.*)

CELIA, *suddenly upset, gets up, runs to him.*

CELIA. Oh, darling, I was just being silly, just playing games. I didn't think for a minute you'd believe – and – and – I'm sorry, darling, I'm sorry, there, there. Just a silly game, that's all. Between us.

The doorbell rings.

CELIA (*stepping away*). Oh, there he is, your Mr Thing, I'll let him in, darling, you'd better blow your nose and – (*Going towards door.*) what's his name again? Oh, I remember. (*Goes out.*)

Sound of front door opening.

CELIA (*off*). Good evening, Mr Ambrose. He's in there waiting for you, he's been practising all afternoon –

HOLLY *hurries to the piano.*

CELIA *enters, followed by* BROWNLOW.

CELIA. There, you see. Warming the keys and finger tips.

BROWNLOW. Good evening, Holliday.

HOLLY (*getting up*). Good evening, sir.

BROWNLOW. No, don't be up, put yourself back where you're going to be for the next hour.

CELIA. I'm so glad to have caught you for once, Mr Ambrose, I always seem to be out or dashing off just as you arrive, it's usually my tennis hour, you see, but I do hope Holly thinks to offer you a cup of tea, do you, Holly?

HOLLY. What, Mummy?

CELIA. Do you think to offer Mr Ambrose a cup of tea, darling?

BROWNLOW. Yes, he does, Mrs Smithers, unfailingly. But I always decline. One has to worry too much about the clinking of cup on saucer. It's Brownlow, by the way.

CELIA (*momentarily confused*). What?

BROWNLOW. Not Ambrose. Ambrose is my middle name.

CELIA (*laughs*). Oh, of course it is, I'm so sorry, I know your name perfectly well, don't I, Holly, it's just that my eye caught Ambrose on the what's-it Holly's playing and it stuck. Well, Mr Brownlow, I'll get out of the way and leave you two to it, shall I?

BROWNLOW. Mrs Smithers, may I ask a favour? I'd be grateful if you'd let me take the telephone off the hook. Its ringing can be very disruptive, we've discovered.

CELIA. The telephone? Oh, but there are sometimes calls for my husband. From the hospital, you see. When they want him urgently. He's the pathologist, after all. The only pathologist, you know.

BROWNLOW. Indeed I do know. And I'm sorry, I wouldn't have dreamt of asking if I'd known Dr Smithers was in the house.

CELIA. Well, he isn't, as a matter of fact. So I suppose, now I come to think of it – (*Going reluctantly to the telephone.*) and I'm not expecting anything myself that can't wait.

BROWNLOW. They always come when they come, at the worst possible time. And once one has come, one expects others to follow. The hour becomes about whether the telephone is going to ring and not about the piano. Which is why I refuse to have one in my house.

CELIA. Yes, I do understand. But we must remember to put it back when you've finished. In case my husband needs to call me urgently – well, if he's going to be home late or –

BROWNLOW. We will remember, I promise you.

CELIA. Thank you. Well, then. (*Goes out.*)

There is a pause.

BROWNLOW (*as if to himself*). Well, here we are again. Just the two of us, surrounded by the foe. And visible this time. (*To* HOLLY.) But how nice to have had a proper little conversation with your mother. How have you been getting on with my what's-it?

HOLLY. Sir?

BROWNLOW. Mr Ambrose's what's-it. Have you come to love it yet?

HOLLY. I like it a lot.

BROWNLOW. You're developing a feeling for it then, are you?

HOLLY. It gets easier and easier the more I get to know it.

BROWNLOW. Ah. Then you're not developing a feeling for it. It should get more and more complicated the more you get to know it. You'll only know it completely when you come to realise that you're never going to find out its secret. Perhaps because there isn't one. (*Laughs.*) I'm teasing you, mio. That's the way I'd like people to talk about my music. As they don't I have to do it myself, and so I make it preposterous to myself. Especially when I do it to that. It's merely a finger exercise to make you more agile. Your fingers anyway. (*Surveys* HOLLY.) What a strange posture. You look as if you're crouching for a sprint. Waiting for the gun to go off. Turn around, if you please.

HOLLY *turns around.*

BROWNLOW. Back straight, if you please.

HOLLY *straightens his back.*

BROWNLOW. Arms out, fingers ready.

HOLLY *stretches out his arms, hooks his fingers.*

BROWNLOW. No, no, you're not going to savage the keyboard, you're going to caress it, if you please. There. (*Makes caressing movements with his own hands. Little pause.*) If you please, mio.

HOLLY *begins to make caressing movements with his hands. For a moment they are both making caressing movements.*

BROWNLOW. Now. Oh, one thing.

HOLLY. Sir?

BROWNLOW. Who is this 'sir' you keep referring to? I thought we'd got rid of him weeks ago.

HOLLY. Sorry, Lowly. (*In a mutter.*)

BROWNLOW. You're quite safe. They may be all around us but they're not actually with us. Nobody can hear you except me. Say it again without the apology.

HOLLY. Lowly.

BROWNLOW. That's better. Once more. (*Puts his hand on HOLLY's cheek.*)

HOLLY. Lowly.

BROWNLOW. Now explain to me why we decided you should call me Lowly.

HOLLY. Because you have low aspirations or why would you be bothering with creatures like me.

BROWNLOW. Did I say that?

HOLLY. I think so. I think that's what you said.

BROWNLOW. Well, now I shan't be able to remember whether I said it or not. I'll just remember what you said I said and hope that it was really I and not actually you that said it.

HOLLY. It was, Lowly, I promise.

BROWNLOW (*taking his hand from HOLLY's cheek*). Now, mio, to Lowly's Bagatelle, if you please. Unless you have a greater aspiration.

HOLLY *turns to keyboard, begins to play Bagatelle.*

BROWNLOW *stands, listening to music. Lets out a groan. Stands in a posture of despair.*

HOLLY (*turns slowly*). Did I make a mistake?

BROWNLOW. No. I did. (*Goes over, takes score off music stand, looks at it.*)

HOLLY. Don't you like it any more?

BROWNLOW. You play it as if I never liked it, mio.

HOLLY. I'm sorry. I do like it. Honestly.

BROWNLOW. Thank you. (*Stuffs score into his pocket.*) Play something more worthy of your gifts, if you please. (*Riffling through scores on piano, picking one out.*) Here, play this. (*Puts score on music stand.*) At least we'll know where we are.

HOLLY *begins to play opening bars of the 'Moonlight' sonata.*

BROWNLOW *puts his hands in his pockets, walks around the room, nodding his head, staring at* HOLLY.

There is a sudden slight discord. BROWNLOW *winces.* HOLLY *proceeds to play.*

BROWNLOW (*hissing it out*). Stop! Stop, stop, stop!

HOLLY *stops.*

BROWNLOW. Didn't you hear yourself?

HOLLY *nods.*

BROWNLOW. Then why didn't you stop yourself? How do you expect to learn, mio, if you simply ignore your mistakes? Mistakes bury themselves into our natures. They become habits we don't even know we possess. So we must be alert to them, ready to correct them – turn to our teachers for help. That's what I'm here for, aren't I? To help. Answer, if you please. Without mumbling. And no, don't turn.

HOLLY. Yes, sir. (*Pipingly.*)

BROWNLOW. Yes who, mio? (*Gently.*)

HOLLY. Lowly, sir. I mean Lowly, I mean.

BROWNLOW. And to what, mio?

HOLLY. To help, Lowly. (*Pause.* BROWNLOW *waits.*) That's what you're here for. (*Pause.*) To help with your mistakes. My mistakes I mean, sir. Lowly.

BROWNLOW (*lets out a little laugh*). Who can say whether the man is playing with the cat or the cat is playing with the man? Eh? (*Goes over to piano.*) Move over, mio. (*Sits beside* HOLLY.) Now watch my hands. (*Begins to play.*)

He has a velvet touch, his head moves very slightly to the music. He stops, nods at the keyboard and at HOLLY. HOLLY *starts again.*

BROWNLOW *at first watches his hands, then as if against his will, turns, stares at* HOLLY's *profile. With an effort, he gets up, walks softly around the room, and as* HOLLY *reaches the point of the previous discord, passes it successfully,* BROWNLOW *nods to himself. Stares towards* HOLLY, *rapt.*

CELIA *enters room, makes to speak.* BROWNLOW *puts his finger to his lips.*

BROWNLOW (*after a moment, gently*). Holly. (HOLLY *stops.*) I think your mother wants a word.

CELIA. I'm so sorry to interrupt, such lovely sounds and such a gorgeous piece of music, what a lucky cat! But I've got to make – I've really got to make one telephone call, very important or the whole evening will be a shambles, I'll be very quick, I promise. (*Going to telephone, lighting a cigarette as she does so. Goes through telephone book.*) M – M – M – M – M – here we are. (*Dials.*) Well, fingers crossed. (*Holds out her fingers crossed, smiles at* BROWNLOW. *On telephone.*) Mrs Milton? It's Mrs Smithers here, Dr Smithers's wife – how are you? Oh dear, how unpleasant. I think there's something going around the island, I was going to play tennis with Mrs Authwaite but she had to call it off because she's got exactly the same – runny eyes, sniffles, a slight temperature – my husband always says that they are just little upsets and there's nothing you can do about them really, but you know the famous saying about doctors and their families – um, what I'm 'phoning about is that when I bumped into you in the village the other day you very sweetly said that sometimes your chickens did you really proud and if ever I were in desperate need it's always worth giving you a ring, so you wouldn't by any chance – oh, you have, how wonderful! Well, I was hoping four – three, I see. Well, I can make do on three, that's very kind of you, the doctor will be pleased, he's been longing for a freshly made omelette. He'll pick them up himself on his way back from the hospital, I'll 'phone him and tell him straight away – thank you, Mrs Milton. (*Puts down telephone.*) Isn't it revolting how obsequious we have to be these days? Especially with the Mrs Miltons of the world. They don't do you kindnesses, you know, they do you favours – (*Dialling as she speaks. On telephone.*) Oh hello, Dr Smithers, Path Lab, please. (*Pause.*) Laboratory. Pathological Laboratory. (*Irritated.*) This is Mrs Smithers, Dr Smithers's wife – oh, Jean, hello, Jean, Celia Smithers here, can I just have a word? Oh, doing a post mortem, I see – well, Jean my dear, would you just give him this message – to stop off at Mrs Milton's on the way home and pick up –

Sound of front door opening and closing.

CELIA. Good heavens, who's that?

CHARLES SMITHERS *enters.*

CELIA. My dear, what are you doing here, I'm on the 'phone to you, I mean leaving you a message about picking up the eggs –

CHARLES. I tried to 'phone to let you know I was on my way but the line was constantly engaged.

CELIA. What? Oh yes, (*Remembering telephone.*) well, Mr Brown, he likes to have the 'phone off the hook – (*On telephone.*) it's all right, Jean dear, he's here –

CHARLES. No, don't hang up, let me have a word.

CELIA (*on telephone*). Hang on, Jean dear, he wants a word. (*Handing 'phone to CHARLES.*)

CHARLES (*on telephone*). Oh hello, Jean. Bad case of the
  Gremlins again downstairs, Greatorix says he'll have it
  sorted out by eight and knowing young Greatorix he will.
  Thank you, Jean. (*Hangs up.*)

CELIA. You're not going to have to go back tonight, darling?

CHARLES. I hope not. Sounds clear cut enough. A drowning.
  There shouldn't be any urgency.

CELIA. A drowning, oh dear. One of the fishermen, I suppose
  – oh darling, this is Mr – (*Gestures.*) Holly's piano teacher,
  you haven't met, have you?

CHARLES (*nods*). How do you do?

BROWNLOW (*coming forward, hand held out*). How do you
  do, Dr Smithers, how do you do?

They shake hands.

CELIA (*sotto voce to* HOLLY). Holly, do turn around. There
  are people in the room.

HOLLY *turns, gets up.*

CHARLES. Well, do stay and – and have a drink. (*Gestures.*)

BROWNLOW. How very kind of you, but I really mustn't use
  up any of your valuable time being sociable.

CHARLES (*surprised*). My time isn't at all valuable. Anyway
  now I'm at home.

CELIA. I think, darling, Mr Brown – um – is thinking about
  Holly's lesson. They're right in the middle, you see. Perhaps
  we should have our drinks in the kitchen – oh, but first
  could my husband hear Holly play the thing you wrote for
  your cat?

BROWNLOW. It's not so much a thing as a bagatelle. (*Smiling
  politely.*)

CELIA. It sounds very advanced – at least to my ear – but then
  I've got a tin ear, as you've probably guessed.

BROWNLOW. It is quite advanced. But then so is your son.
  (*Little bow.*)

CELIA (*to* HOLLY). There, you see, what did I tell you? Straight from the horse's mouth – and all your talk about violins!

BROWNLOW. Violins?

CELIA. Yes, yes, he was full of one of his nonsenses about giving up football and the piano so he could go to Portsmouth to take lessons with goodness knows who.

BROWNLOW *looks at* HOLLY. *There is a silence.*

HOLLY. Oh, Mummy, I didn't mean I wanted to give up the piano exactly – I like the piano – but I'd like to know more about the violin.

BROWNLOW. I can show you whatever it is you think you'd like to know about the violin.

CELIA. There you are, you see? Everything you want without giving up anything.

CHARLES. I'm afraid I'm a little lost in all this.

CELIA. Oh, don't worry about it, darling, we'll just listen to Holly for a minute and then go and have our drinks in the kitchen.

BROWNLOW. Well then, Holliday. Perform, please.

HOLLY *begins to play the 'Moonlight' sonata.*

BROWNLOW. Ah, we forgot to change the sheets. (*Puts his hand in his pocket, checks himself.*) Why don't you try it from memory, make a little test out of it?

HOLLY *begins to play the Bagatelle, then starts to encounter difficulties.*

CELIA *and* CHARLES *listen, smiling politely, unaware.*

BROWNLOW. Thank you, Holliday. (*Unable to suppress sharpness.*)

HOLLY *stops.*

BROWNLOW (*recovering*). Just entering a very treacherous patch – unless you know it by heart – and even then –

CELIA. Still, it was lovely, wasn't it, darling?

CHARLES. Very impressive, very impressive. And you wrote it yourself?

CELIA (*to* CHARLES). They're going to do it on the Third Programme, Holly was telling me. We must make a point of listening, darling.

CHARLES. Yes, do let us know when.

CELIA. Yes, please do. Well, I'll just pour us our drinks (*Going to drinks table.*) and we'll be off to the kitchen and – oh, darling, we mustn't forget this whole thing about Mrs Milton.

CHARLES. Mrs Milton? What does she want?

CELIA. I'm afraid, darling, it's what we want – it's some eggs that I said you were going to pick up on the way back.

CHARLES. Oh, I'll drive over in a minute.

CELIA. No, no, that's not fair, you want to put your feet up, especially if you have to go out again, (*Pouring drinks.*) I'll peddle over – or Holly even, won't take him a minute with his young legs – what was it you said the other day (*To* HOLLY.) when I told you to go and fetch something and your legs were so much younger than mine – and you said – he said (*Coming over, putting drink in* CHARLES'*s hand, drink in her own hand.*) – 'Oh, Mummy,' you said, 'Wouldn't it be more sensible to use up the old ones first?' (*Laughs.*)

CHARLES *grunts a laugh.*

BROWNLOW (*laughs*). Very amusing, very amusing.

CHARLES. Are you sure you won't – (*Holding up drink.*)

BROWNLOW. No, no, I think – I really feel that it would be best for me to leave you – (*Gestures.*) you want to be comfortable –

CELIA. No, we can do perfectly well in the kitchen, can't we, darling?

CHARLES. What? Oh, yes. (*Struggles to his feet.*)

BROWNLOW. No, I'll make up the lesson the next time. But what I think would be a very good idea – so that we're not in your way in the future –

CELIA. Oh, you're not usually, it's just that the doctor's been up since seven –

CHARLES. Oh, don't worry about me.

BROWNLOW. Still, one wants one's home to be one's home after a hard day's work, whatever hour one gets back. I don't generally allow my pupils to use my piano but Holly has got such an exceptional touch that he won't be a danger to it. Also I think it's time he got the feel of a – if you will permit me to say so – a more delicate instrument. A more responsive one.

CELIA. Well, that's awfully good of you, Mr – isn't it, Holly darling?

HOLLY. Yes. Yes. Thank you very much, sir.

CHARLES. Will your prep be all right, Holly?

CELIA. Oh yes, his prep. He always has to do his prep before the lesson, it's an absolute rule.

BROWNLOW. He can bring his prep to me. I'll make sure we don't start until he's finished it.

CELIA. Oh. Well, what about his tea?

BROWNLOW. My mother can make him his tea. She'll enjoy having a boy to feed, and it'll only be once or twice a week.

CELIA. Twice a week?

BROWNLOW. Oh – when we get into something special. An extra hour now and then might make all the difference.

CELIA (*to* CHARLES). Is that all right, darling? I mean from the financial point of view?

BROWNLOW. Oh, please don't worry about that. Whenever a bit of extra time comes up it'll be entirely my decision, entirely on my account.

CHARLES. It's very good of you, but won't this interfere with other arrangements – your other pupils, I mean?

BROWNLOW. I haven't got any other pupils, Dr Smithers. I go to a number of boys and girls because their parents feel that their off-spring ought to have some piano lessons, even though they're musical clodhoppers – a social matter, really. Holliday, who has a gift – be assured he has a very considerable gift – is my only pupil in any proper meaning of the word. I consider it a privilege to teach him.

CELIA. And I know he feels the same. He feels it's a privilege to be taught by you. (*Looking at* HOLLY.)

HOLLY. Yes. Yes, thank you, sir.

CHARLES. Well, then. However, I would prefer to pay for all my son's tuition.

BROWNLOW (*does his odd little bow*). Well, we won't quarrel over it, will we, Doctor?

CELIA. Now that's all settled, do stay and have a quick drink.

CHARLES. Yes, have a drink, do have one.

BROWNLOW. No, I've still got time to get to the fishmonger's, they generally keep a few scraps for my mother. Well, for her cat, I mean.

CELIA (*triumphantly*). Oh yes, Miaow.

CHARLES *looks at her. There is a pause.*

CELIA. Miaow. Isn't that the name of your cat, the one you wrote the music for? Didn't you say, Holly?

HOLLY. Yes – yes – mi-oh, really, more than miaow, isn't it, sir?

BROWNLOW. Yes, mi-oh. Mi-oh is my cat's name. I mustn't forget to introduce you. (*To* HOLLY.) I'll be off. (*Makes towards door.*)

CELIA. Holly dear, show Mr Burnham the door.

HOLLY *runs ahead of* BROWNLOW, *opens door.*

BROWNLOW. Thank you, Holliday.

CELIA. Oh, Holly darling, why don't you nip on over to Mrs Milton for the eggs, see if you can't wheedle four out of her?

HOLLY. Right, Mummy. (*Hurries out after* BROWNLOW.)

CHARLES (*settling back*). Thank God.

CELIA. Sssh, darling, he'll hear you. (*Closing sitting room door.*) I suppose it's all right Holly going over there.

CHARLES. A bloody sight better than my coming home and finding him here.

CELIA. He's a very good teacher, everybody says so, lucky to have him on the island. I must be careful, though, with Moira – he does her two, you know – I'm sure she wouldn't enjoy hearing his view of their musical gifts – what did he call them, 'clodhoppers' wasn't it, 'musical clodhoppers'. (*Laughs.*) Just like Moira on the tennis court – she stood me up, you know.

CHARLES. Still, I'm going to pay him for anything extra.

CELIA. But why, darling, if it gives him so much pleasure?

CHARLES. I just feel easier, don't want to be beholden, something about the chap, odd – that handshake. (*Grimaces.*)

CELIA. You don't think he's a Jew, do you?

CHARLES. Could be. Anyway, something slightly off about him.

CELIA. Well of course, a lot of them are very artistic and musical. And at least he's not being a Jew on the money front.

CHARLES. No, but that's another reason for making sure we're all square. All square and straight.

CELIA. Well, let's see what kind of bill he gives us, he hasn't asked for anything yet. (*Comes and sits beside* CHARLES.) Have you had a rotten day, my Chaps? (*Stroking his leg.*)

CHARLES. It's beginning to go away a bit.

CELIA *lights a cigarette, offers it with her mouth to* CHARLES.

CHARLES. May I? (*Takes cigarette.*)

CELIA *lights another for herself.*

CELIA. We'll make it go away completely, Chaps, we will. (*Stroking his forehead.*) You mustn't think about going back tonight to do the drowned man. There's nothing you can do for him that you can't do tomorrow.

CHARLES (*sighs*). Yes, but it isn't a matter of doing for him, it's what there'll be tomorrow as well. Might be wiser to clear him off the decks tonight. As a matter of fact, Ceci, I could have done him this afternoon somehow, could have managed it, but I took advantage of Greatorix not being quite ready – he hadn't finished cleaning the body. So I just left.

CELIA. Well then, you needed to. You would never do that unless you absolutely needed to.

CHARLES. Couldn't face it, you see. Now we're back in civilian life, getting used to things as they used to be, although they never will be quite as they used to be, will they? – it's much harder, the death of young men particularly – boys they were almost at the beginning, weren't they? – three, four, five a day, no time for post mortems, no need for them, just being an ordinary doctor in an air base – broken bones, burnt flesh – so you think you could deal with the occasional corpse, don't even have to see the pain, hear it – nothing to try to save, just cut it open, sort through the organs, water in the lungs and pneumonia, heart failure, stroke, diphtheria, polio, drowning – anyway, this afternoon quite suddenly I couldn't face it. (*Little pause.*) That's all I mean.

CELIA. Here, come here. (*Takes his cigarette, stubs it out, stubs out hers, puts drinks on table.*) Come on, my Chaps, lay your head.

CHARLES *puts his head on her breast, she strokes the back of his head.*

CELIA. You stay here tonight. You stay here in your family, safe and sound, where you belong. (*Rocks him gently.*)

CHARLES *lifts his head. They stare into each other's eyes, caress each other's cheeks, kiss gently, then passionately.* CELIA *puts her hand between his legs.*

CELIA. We'll go to bed early and we'll play.

CHARLES. Oh, of course. You haven't had your tennis.

CELIA. Jolly good thing too. It's saved me for you. Mmmm – (*Feels him.*)

CHARLES. I must try to be worth your saving yourself for.

CELIA. You're always that, Chaps. Oh, my man!

CHARLES. Yes, your man. Completely and absolutely yours.

CELIA. That reminds me – *this* reminds me (*Laughs, putting her hand between his legs again.* CHARLES *puts his hand on top of hers.*) Holly.

CHARLES. What?

CELIA. Well, he's started.

CHARLES. Started what? Oh!

CELIA. Though actually, my dear, I don't think 'started' is quite the word. I sometimes wonder if he ever stops. His sheets every morning – I thought something was up when he began making his bed so tight.

CHARLES. You've been carrying out inspections then, have you?

CELIA. I do change the sheets, you know, darling. Inevitably, as I do all the housework. Anyway, it's not a question of inspections, I couldn't avoid it even if I tried – the other day he shot into the house and rushed upstairs saying he had to get some prep done before tea, and when I put my head around the door to make sure he was really at it – well, there he was, on his knees, can you believe?

CHARLES. On his knees? Well, that's rather bold.

CELIA. What do you mean?

CHARLES. Well, on his knees in his bedroom and you likely to come in at any minute – that's rather bold in my book.

CELIA. Well, he wasn't actually unbuttoned, and he pretended he was praying, he had his palms pressed in front of his face like this – (*Does it.*) and his eyes closed, but I could see some wretched-looking magazine under one knee and a piece of paper under the other one.

CHARLES. What did you say?

CELIA. Nothing, of course. Well, except that I was sorry I'd interrupted him at his devotions. Then at tea I said, darling, if you're becoming religious there's always church, you know, on Sundays.

CHARLES (*laughs*). And what did he say?

CELIA. That at the moment he wanted to keep it between himself and his God.

CHARLES. That's rather a fine way of putting it.

CELIA. But seriously, darling – I know it's silly but I can't help it – I do rather hate the feeling that it's going on, you see. Furtively. Shamefully. And lying about it. It makes it all so nasty.

CHARLES. Well, it's better, surely, than having him doing it openly and publicly and boasting about it, darling.

CELIA. Oh, don't be a fool, Charles! (*Laughing in spite of herself.*) But don't you think you ought to have a little talk with him? Let him know that what he's going through is all perfectly natural and normal and – and nothing to be, well, ashamed of. That's what we're meant to do, isn't it, these days in the 1950s – or you, anyway, as a father – be open and honest. And – and natural.

CHARLES *laughs.*

CELIA. What?

CHARLES. I'm just thinking of my father being open, honest and natural with me, just think of him! 'Charles, after a great deal of thought and consultation with your mother and my colleagues, I have decided that the time has come to discuss with you certain matters connected to the procreation of the species. Not just in general terms but in specific. Indeed, personal ones. As you know, your mother and I always believed that both at school and at home it is of the utmost importance that you keep, in the eyes of the world, a clean sheet' – (*Bursts out laughing.*)

CELIA (*laughing*). But he probably didn't know what you were up to, or if he did, pretended to himself he didn't. Darling, if we had a daughter I wouldn't think twice about doing it myself. Anyway, I've told him.

CHARLES. Told him what?

CELIA. That you're going to have a talk with him.

CHARLES. Oh, God, you haven't! What on earth got into you?

CELIA. Well, it was really the thought of those magazines, you see. They may be absolutely foul and corrupting for all we know. They may even be against the law. And whatever it is he's been writing, it's been getting in the way of his prep – that's the point, Charles, we don't want him getting muddled and confused and carried away with his scholarship coming up. (*Picks up* HOLLY*'s satchel, begins to go through it.*)

CHARLES (*noticing* CELIA *and satchel*). Really, darling, I'm not sure we have the right –

CELIA. Ah, here you are. (*Triumphantly produces magazine, hands it to* CHARLES.) 'Nature Today'.

CHARLES (*taking magazine, looking at it*). 'A magazine for naturalists' – oh, I see, for nudists. (*Flicking through it.*) Photographs of nudists – rather fleshy – still, young – oh, here's one that's quite pretty – (*Showing picture to* CELIA, *who has found exercise book, taken out loose pages.*) anyway, nothing that qualifies as corrupting or foul or illegal. A perfectly reasonable way of finding out what a naked woman looks like, surely.

CELIA. But there's this.

CHARLES. What is it?

CELIA. I don't know, I haven't looked, I don't want to – here. (*Hands him loose sheet.*)

CHARLES (*takes sheet*). It really does seem wrong, quite wrong – (*Muttering, as he reads sheet of paper.*)

CELIA *lights a cigarette.*

CHARLES (*shakes his head*). It's just about some girl he's been peeking at, or imagining he's been peeking at, under water – describing her nipples – and trying to see between her legs. (*Looks up.*) I used to write stuff like this, though actually not as good – well, as literary – and I can remember a time when I didn't know what was between a girl's legs either. Actually, I think I supposed it was rather like what I had between my own legs, only much smaller and daintier, more feminine in other words.

CELIA. Well, there you are. You can set him right about that, for one thing.

CHARLES (*bursts out*). Would you like to help? Be the demonstrator's model?

CELIA (*genuinely shocked*). Charles! What on earth's got into you!

There is a pause.

CHARLES. Sorry, darling, sorry, I – I – it's just the thought of – of –

Sound of door opening.

CHARLES. Oh, God!

CELIA. Quick, here, give it to me!

CHARLES *hands* CELIA *magazine and page. She crams them into satchel, pushes satchel down as they assume unnaturally natural positions as* HOLLY *enters, holding brown bag.*

CELIA. Ah, here you are, darling, we were wondering where you'd been all this time.

HOLLY. Mr Brownlow asked me to walk to the village with him. And then I went and got the eggs. Egg, I mean. (*Takes in satchel is upside down in different place.*)

CELIA. Egg? What do you mean, egg?

HOLLY. Well, that's all she had. Just the one left, she said.

CELIA. But didn't you tell her that we need four – at least four – and she promised me three anyway for the doctor's omelette? Didn't you say that, Holly?

HOLLY. Well, no, I just said I'd come for the eggs and she handed me this. And I said I thought there'd be more and she said, well, she was very sorry, there weren't, that's all she had left. (*Hands bag to* CELIA.)

CELIA. Really, this island, these people! And to think how I grovelled to her! You should have gone straight there, Holly, instead of going to the village with Mr – (*Gestures.*) well, we'll just have to make up with the usual powdered, I'm afraid, darling (*To* CHARLES), I'll get started straight away and you two chaps have a little chat, why don't you? (*Gives a quick meaningful look to* CHARLES, *goes out.*)

CHARLES. Don't tell your mother but actually I've come to prefer dried eggs.

HOLLY. So do I.

There is a pause.

HOLLY. Well, I ought to go upstairs with my prep. (*Going to satchel.*)

CHARLES. Not finished yet then?

HOLLY. All but a little bit of French.

CHARLES. Well, why don't you – why don't you sit down and – for a minute or two? I'm sure that can wait. (*Nods to satchel, realises, lets out a little laugh which he converts into a cough.*) For a minute or two.

HOLLY *sits down, clasping satchel to his lap.*

CHARLES. So what did you talk about?

HOLLY. Daddy?

CHARLES. You and Mr – your piano chap. On the way to the village.

HOLLY. Oh, just about the piano, really. And music. And the violin. (*Little pause.*) Nothing.

CHARLES. You obviously get on with him.

HOLLY. Yes, well, he's very good.

CHARLES. I often wonder where you get your musical gifts from. Not from my side of the family – at least as far as I know. Oh, there was a great-uncle, your great-great uncle – Cedric, I think it was, is said to have played the fiddle – but only jigs, and that kind of thing, to please the ladies, I suspect. He was a shameless philanderer, you know. A bit of a gay dog is what that means. A gay old dog, your great-great uncle Cedric. Well, that's the family mythology anyway. But on your mother's side – well, your mother says she doesn't know of anyone at all on her side to account for you – of course she's almost completely tone deaf, isn't she? Although I'm not actually tone deaf myself – I mean I can carry a tune – but the fact is, apart from great uncle Cedric, if it was Cedric who fiddled and jigged, we don't know of anyone on either side – (*Gestures.*) but of course that's the thing about a gene, isn't it, just bobs up generations after it was last seen or heard of. So you're what is known as a sport.

HOLLY. Oh.

CHARLES. It's the word in genetics for what you are. A sudden resurgent gene.

HOLLY. Ah.

CHARLES. Well, everything seems to be going well then? You mustn't let this business of a scholarship weigh you down, you know, if you do get one – but on the other hand, if you don't, you don't.

HOLLY. Mummy says if I don't get one we won't be able to go to London.

CHARLES. Does she? I think you must have misunderstood her. Going to London depends on a great deal of other things, not the least of which whether I can get a job in London. Besides, we may not want to go to London. We may end up somewhere else entirely – here, for instance – or Australia, or South Africa, Canada or New Zealand. Or London.

HOLLY. Oh.

CHARLES. All I'm saying is that it's not the end of the world if you don't get your scholarship, that's all I'm saying. I'm sure your mother would agree. All right?

HOLLY. Thank you, Daddy.

There is a pause.

HOLLY. Well then, I'll just – (*Makes to get up.*)

CHARLES. There's one other thing. It's nothing very – it's not at all – well, Holly, there are some things in life, you know – well, there comes a time – well, of course there are some things in life, what do I mean there are some things in life? Life is full of some things or other things – some things and other things fill our lives every moment of the day, every second. The point is – well, there comes a time between people – well, father and son – when they need to be (*Thinks.*) talked about. Mmm?

HOLLY. Yes, Daddy.

CHARLES. I wish, you know, that your grandfather had found a way of talking to me. Of talking to me as I'm talking to you now. But then – of course you never met my father, did you?

HOLLY. No, Daddy. Well, I suppose I did but he died when I was two, wasn't it, Mummy says.

CHARLES. Somewhere about that time it would have been, yes. Anyway, before you were old enough to get a real sense of him. But then I'm not sure I ever got a real sense of him. And he died when I was thirty-three. (*Laughs ruefully.*) I don't mean he was mysterious or there was some dark secret – no, no, not at all. I knew what he did. Like me he was a doctor, though not a pathologist. A straight forward general practitioner is what he was, so of course he knew how to talk to his patients – naturally I don't have to know how to talk to my patients as they're usually dead, although they talk to me in what I discover in this diseased organ or that, samples of tissue – I hear them through my microscope. (*Little pause.*) I've never really discussed my work with you before, have I?

HOLLY. No, Daddy.

CHARLES. What do you know about it?

HOLLY. Well, only that you find out why people died. Isn't that it?

CHARLES (*after a little pause*). Yes. That's it, old chap. Why people died. There's always a scientific explanation, even if I can't always find it. If I had my time again I'd go into psychiatry, all the patients alive and talking for themselves, that's where the medical future lies – financially anyway – and I wouldn't have to put up with all this death – I mean death is – is – (*Frowns, looks into his drink as if lost.*) Do you know what a psychiatrist is?

HOLLY. Well, no, not really, Daddy.

CHARLES. Well, let's hope you never have to find out, eh? (*Laughs.*)

HOLLY *laughs. There is a little pause.*

CHARLES. Oh, by the way, that reminds me. Girls, old chap. Do you ever find yourself, um, noticing them? Thinking about them?

HOLLY. No, Daddy. Not really. (*Shaking his head.*)

CHARLES. Never?

HOLLY. Well, sometimes – a little bit, I suppose.

CHARLES. Well, I'm glad to hear it. Because otherwise there would be – well, frankly, something odd. (*Takes a sip of scotch, tries not to look as if he's bracing himself.*) Um, masturbation, old boy?

The telephone rings.

CHARLES. Oh, blast! (*Picks up telephone.*) Hayling 349? Greatorix – oh hello, you're still there, are you, how are you getting on?

As HOLLY *gets up, gestures tentatively as he goes out.* CHARLES *lifts his hand in vague salute.*

CHARLES (*on telephone*). Mmmhm. Ah. So you think I'd better come over tonight?

CELIA *enters.*

CHARLES (*on telephone*). Well, I'd like to eat first if the deceased doesn't mind. (*Smiles at* CELIA.) It's a damn nuisance, I was looking forward to an evening at home – (*Hangs up.*)

CELIA. Poor darling. (*Pats him on the cheek.*)

CHARLES. Well, we had that little talk you wanted. And I'm happy to report it's all just as I said it would be – normal. Perfectly normal at his age.

CELIA. There, I knew it would be. So why you had to make such a fuss about a simple little father/son chat! (*Goes to door.*) Holly? Holly darling, it's supper – hurry, because your father's got to be off. (*To* CHARLES.) I wish it wasn't mainly powdered eggs but there, I'll put the fresh one in your bit for being such a dear old Chaps.

Lights.

Scene Three

Three months later. Late afternoon. Summer.

BROWNLOW*'s study/sitting room.*

HOLLY *is sitting at the table, satchel beside him, writing, consulting the dictionary.*

MRS BROWNLOW (ELLIE) *enters, carrying a tray of tea, on which also a bottle of sherry and a glass.* ELLIE *drinks sherry steadily throughout the following scene.*

ELLIE (*has a Viennese accent*). Come on, Catty-Kit, come on, Catty-Kit, puss, puss, puss, come on – (*Puts tray down on table. Pours herself a glass of sherry. To* HOLLY.) Are you finished?

HOLLY. Yes, I have. I was just checking some words. (*Closing dictionary.*)

ELLIE. Good, good, once more I have the right time, I seem always to know, yes? (*Rumples* HOLLY*'s hair, goes to door.*) Catty-Kit, Catty-Kit, puss, puss – don't be frightened of him, he's a very kind boy, he will not hurt you – (*Bends down.*) ooh – ooh, Catty-Kit – ooh, come to Mama – oh, silly! Silly frightened thing! (*Stands up, shuts the door.*) It is no good, when you are here she will not come. You must not think it is personal with you, she is not in the habit of guests, you see. We don't have many guests so she thinks you are an intruder, come to take her place even. But still I should leave the door open in case she changes her mind and wishes to be a friend with you at last. Now, here, let us have our tea. (*Lifting lids.*) We have two boiled eggs, we have toast and we have – here, Sachertorte. This is a very special cake we make in Vienna. Before the war it was famous everywhere. Now of course I do not know whether they can still make Sachertorte, it is difficult enough to do it on the island with so little chocolate, but we do not complain because here we have our Sachertorte whether they have it or do not have it any more in Vienna. Eat please. Eat, Holliday. (*Claps her hands.*) Why must I always tell you to start? Is it that you are shy eating alone with me? (*Pouring him a cup of tea.*) Here, your cuppa, your nice English cuppa. Now you will feel safe and comfortable with your nice English cuppa. You have such good manners, how is the egg?

HOLLY (*swallowing egg*). Very nice, thank you, Ellie.

ELLIE. My boy also has very good manners. But not with me. Never with me. He always makes fun from me – even as a baby he was making fun from me. Do you make fun from your mutter?

HOLLY. Not really.

ELLIE. Then you have a father and he won't permit you. So lucky mutter. My boy was never with a father. Dead before he was born. Did he tell you that?

HOLLY. No, Ellie.

ELLIE. He was not a young man, my Emil, but he was very big, very strong. He had a bad heart, you see. A man of good heart with a bad heart. And sometimes he was angry, very angry. I think he would have been angry with my boy quite often. He was not an artist, he was a banker. And a soldier. Brave. What is it like today outside? Catty-Kit, Catty-Kit – I thought I felt her, did you see her? Was she there?

HOLLY. No, I didn't see her.

ELLIE (*going to window*). It is beautiful outside, I can see that, but is it cold, is there a wind?

HOLLY. Not very cold, Ellie, no. Don't you like going out then?

ELLIE. No, I do not go out.

HOLLY. Never? I mean, don't you ever go out?

ELLIE. No. I stay here, inside, where I have trust, you see. Safety. When I arrive in this house I think, now I will never have to go outside again. It was very bad for me, you see, in Portsmouth, in the war. Because of my accent. Everybody thinks I am a Nazi from the Gestapo. Such silly they think. When I go to shops – it is very terrible for my boy, they think he is a little Nazi Gestapo when I speak. Or black market when I have coupons. Or a Jew even. You, Holliday, do you think we are Jews?

HOLLY. No. I mean, I don't know, I've never thought about it, Ellie.

ELLIE. Of course you have. And your father and your mutter. I know you English, they are always looking very close. So?

HOLLY. I don't think you're Jews, Ellie. Nor do my parents. Well, they've never said, honestly, and I expect they would have said something if they thought you were.

ELLIE. Well, it is true they have only seen my boy. They look at him and they say straight away, no, he is not a Jew. But if they hear my voice – me – my voice, you understand? then they would be confused. But now you can tell them yourself everything about me. Yes, Holliday? You are the only one he brings back to see me, ever. Oh, Teddy sometimes – when we were in London – but he was not his pupil, he is grown up. Like him, poor soul. Grown ups. Hah! Do you know what I mean?

HOLLY *shakes his head.*

ELLIE. That is good. I am glad of that. There must be no trouble. I cannot move again to another house. I will not move. This is my home. This is my last home. Do you understand?

HOLLY. Not really.

ELLIE. That is good. There is nothing for you to understand. What we say is private, yes?

HOLLY *nods.*

ELLIE. You cross your fingers?

HOLLY *nods.*

ELLIE. Well then, cross your fingers.

HOLLY *crosses his fingers.*

ELLIE. You are a little gentleman. Now you shall have some Sachertorte. There. (*Cutting slice, putting it on a plate.*) Eat, please.

HOLLY *makes to pick it up.*

ELLIE. No, no, there is a fork. You must always eat
Sachertorte with a fork, otherwise it is not Sachertorte, it is
only chocolate cake. Now. (*Putting fork into* HOLLY*'s
hand. Stands, watching* HOLLY *as he eats.*) There. What do
you think of Sachertorte?

HOLLY. Oh, it's – very nice, Ellie.

ELLIE. Very nice! All you English, you say that about
everything – everything is always very nice – I am very
nice, you are very nice, we are very nice, the house is very
nice, God himself is very nice – or it's a very nice bomb,
nice gas, nice, nice, nice – England is very, very, very nice –
what a pity it isn't also very, very, very kind, huh? Because
kind is nicer. Much nicer.

There is a pause.

HOLLY. It's delicious. Really delicious.

ELLIE (*claps her hands*). Thank you. Thank you, thank you,
thank you. For that you will have some more.

HOLLY. Oh no, no thank you, Ellie – no, really.

ELLIE. Why not?

HOLLY. Well, if I eat anything more I'll be too full to play the
piano properly.

ELLIE. And my boy will not like that, huh? If you sit there
with a big stomach, playing the piano, (*Does piano
movements with her fingers.*) your stomach – woof – all big
– woof! He is a very good teacher.

HOLLY. Yes.

ELLIE. He is very serious.

HOLLY. Yes.

ELLIE. He is a genius. You don't think so?

HOLLY. Oh yes, yes – I mean I expect he is. I'm sure he is,
Ellie.

ELLIE. One day you will see. I hope only that I live so long, it is my hope. No, it is not my hope. After I am gone, then he can be a genius to all the world. Now he can be my genius and your genius, we keep him to us. Our little secret, eh, Holliday? (*Goes to him, rumples his hair, kisses him.*) Ah, yes, my little English gentleman, we shall have our genius to ourselves, mmm? (*Laughs, caresses him on the cheeks.*) Is he nice to you like me? (*Stares intently down at* HOLLY.) Sssh – (*Picks up bottle of sherry and glass, takes a quick gulp from glass, then puts them behind flowers on table, goes to door, opens it.*) Catty-Kit, Catty-Kit, puss, puss, puss – oh, there you are, back then, we didn't hear you come in.

BROWNLOW *enters, carrying his coat over his arm.*

BROWNLOW. That wasn't me you were calling then, mutti?

ELLIE. What's your name, Catty-Kit, suddenly? (*Taking his coat, putting it on back of chair.*)

BROWNLOW. Ah, Number Seven, you mean. He or she was hurrying out of the kitchen when I came in, carrying something or other between his or her jaws. A mouse, do you think? A mouse, mutti? A mouse, mutti, for Number Seven?

ELLIE. You're teasing me, you're teasing me again, Thomas. (*Slapping at him playfully.*) It wasn't a mouse and it is a girl, you know very well. And her name is Catty-Kit. Why are you back so early, look, he is still drinking his cuppa.

BROWNLOW. The Merrivale twins had colds so I refused to teach them. I went for a walk by the sea and if I'm early (*Glances at his watch*), it's only by five minutes. You haven't practised for me yet then? (*To* HOLLY.)

HOLLY *shakes his head.*

BROWNLOW. Ah.

HOLLY. I was just going to.

BROWNLOW. Were you? (*Fixes him with a look.*)

HOLLY *lowers his eyes, looks away.*

ELLIE. Oh, you mustn't be unkind with him, it is my fault,
I was talking and talking and talking.

BROWNLOW. Now, mutti, you can stop talking and talking
and talking and let us get on with our work.

ELLIE. You be kind to him, he is a good boy.

BROWNLOW. Yes, I know. A little gentleman, isn't he?
(*Turning* ELLIE *around.*) Go, mutti, and do the washing up.

ELLIE (*as she goes out*). Ah, there you are, waiting for me,
come –

BROWNLOW *closes the door.*

BROWNLOW. Where did she put it this time?

HOLLY. Behind the flowers.

BROWNLOW *goes to flowers, takes bottle of sherry, raises
it, studies it.*

BROWNLOW (*still holding bottle of sherry*). I trust you keep
all our little family secrets to yourself, mio.

HOLLY. Of course I do, Lowly.

BROWNLOW. Because never forget, they're your family
secrets too now, aren't they? What was she talking and
talking and talking about this time?

HOLLY. The same as last time, really, and the time before.
What she always talks about. Though I never quite
understand it, really.

BROWNLOW (*sits in armchair, puts bottle of sherry on floor
beside him*). And what do you tell them when you go home,
about what transpires here – our transpirations here? Mmm?

HOLLY. Nothing.

BROWNLOW. They don't ask questions then?

HOLLY. Well, only the first time. About what I had for tea,
mainly, and what Ellie was like – what your mother was
like. I said they were both very nice. That's all. They
haven't asked anything since.

BROWNLOW. Secrets, secrets. So much of our life is spent
not saying who we are, what we really do, what we really
think. (*Little pause.*) What we really feel. We live in secret
almost all the time. When I was walking along the shore, I
listened to the waves and the wind, the cries of the seagulls,
and I thought – I thought – here, mio, here mio, come on.
(*Pats his lap.*)

HOLLY *goes over, sits on* BROWNLOW's *lap, stiffly.*

BROWNLOW. And I thought – what did I think? That if I
were Bach or Brahms or Mozart or Beethoven, I would hear
so many different sounds – the deep movement of the sea,
the soft wind – how it can become a scream – and the
seagulls, within their ugly shrieks I would hear other songs,
sad songs, of restless souls, whatever, whatever, whatever –
I thought I am not Brahms or Beethoven, I can only
imagine what they might imagine, and do I even want to
hear it, what their imaginings want to hear? Not Ludovic
van Beethoven but Thomas Ambrose Brownlow – well,
Thomas Ambrose Brownlow, what do you really want to
hear? Do you want to know, mio, what I really wanted to
hear?

HOLLY. Yes, Lowly.

BROWNLOW. Yes, mio – yes, Lowly. (*Little pause.*) That's
what I truly wanted to hear. Your voice saying 'Yes, Lowly'.
So. So. Perhaps you will have to be my muse. Perhaps you
are already my muse. But then – but then we have a
contradiction, haven't we? A paradox. Why – why, if you
are my muse, do you make me feel impotent? Do you know
what impotent means?

HOLLY. It means not being able to.

BROWNLOW. And of course you know what a paradox is.

HOLLY. I think so.

BROWNLOW. What is it, mio? What is a paradox?

HOLLY. It's one of the ways you say things when you want to
show off.

BROWNLOW (*laughs shakily*). You are very clever. Am I the only person who knows how clever you are, mio?

HOLLY. I don't know. They think I am at school, I think.

BROWNLOW. And do they ever punish you for it?

HOLLY. No. Why should they?

BROWNLOW. Ah, so another duty falls on me. I will punish you for your cleverness.

HOLLY (*after a pause*). Why?

BROWNLOW (*coldly*). Yours not to reason why, little Englishman. (*Pushing* HOLLY *off his knee.*) Go and stand there – there, by the piano. Now, you know what to do.

HOLLY. But it's not – it's not –

BROWNLOW. And you know what not to do. (*Stares at* HOLLY.)

HOLLY *stands to attention, raises his arms, facing* BROWNLOW.

BROWNLOW. It is through the punishment that we shall find the sin. Another paradox. A paradox that will be received this time in silent respect, not to say humility. A becoming humility. (*After a pause.*) What am I to do, mio, if the muse I need so much is a bad muse? A muse who takes away my power. (*Staring fixedly at* HOLLY *through this.*) You see, this is not showing off, this is giving up my secret. That's what my bad muse makes me do, give up my secret.

Door opens. ELLIE *enters.*

ELLIE. Excuse me please, I'm so sorry, but how can I wash the dishes if I do not have dishes to wash? (*Crosses room. Looks at* HOLLY.) What are you doing, is this a new exercise? Is he teaching you a new trick? (*Groping behind flowers on table.*) What is he doing? (*Sees sherry bottle beside* BROWNLOW.) He mustn't stand like that too long, the blood will leave his hands, then how can he play the piano? (*Picks up tray.*) Put it on the tray, please.

BROWNLOW (*in German*). Go away, mutti, no more for you until tonight.

ELLIE (*in German, hissingly*). And what about you, I know what you're up to, you will cause us trouble again, you will be in disgrace, we'll have to leave – give me the bottle, give me the bottle!

BROWNLOW *puts bottle of sherry on tray.*

ELLIE (*in English*). Thank you. (*In German.*) But for God's sake be careful, control yourself, you must. (*Goes out, leaving door open.*)

BROWNLOW *gets up, goes to door, closes it. Looks at HOLLY, goes over to him, takes handkerchief out of his pocket.*

BROWNLOW. That was very good. Well done, mio. You didn't move your eyes, even though they were running. (*Wipes HOLLY's cheeks.*)

HOLLY *makes to lower his arms.*

BROWNLOW. A minute more, that's all. Let's have a minute more. You can manage that, I know you can. And then you'll have earned your chance with my (*Going to piano, playing.*) beloved. As you stand there think how privileged you are and tell yourself (*Still playing.*) that you must talk to him as I talk to him. Then perhaps he will talk to you as he talks to me. Eh, mio? (*Turns, looks at HOLLY. (Suddenly begins to wheeze.*) Quickly – quickly –

HOLLY *runs to jacket, fumbles in pockets for inhaler.*

As he does so, doorbell over, not noticed by BROWNLOW and HOLLY.

HOLLY *comes over, squirts inhaler into BROWNLOW's mouth in a practised manner as:*

ELLIE (*loud, over*). They're not playing the piano so it will be all right, I'm sure it will be all right – (*Warningly.*) Thomas! Thomas! (*Opening door.*) There's someone to see you, it's the mutter.

BROWNLOW *breathes in, still wheezing, beginning to recover.*

CELIA *enters.*

CELIA. What on earth is going on?

HOLLY. Mr Brownlow, he's having an attack, Mummy.

CELIA. What of?

ELLIE. Oh, it's his asthma. I always tell him he must not get excited.

CELIA. Oh. Are you all right?

BROWNLOW (*squirting inhaler, breathing in, recovering*). Yes – thank you. Thanks to your son's quick thinking. I left this (*Indicating inhaler.*) over there. I should always have it on me. (*Getting up.*) There. Mrs Smithers.

CELIA. Well, I just came – I couldn't resist coming, I wanted him to have the news straight away. He's won a full scholarship to Westminster. Congratulations, Holly. (*Shaking* HOLLY's *hand.*)

HOLLY. Thank you, Mummy.

BROWNLOW. Indeed, indeed congratulations, my boy. (*Shaking* HOLLY's *hand.*)

HOLLY. Thank you, Lowly – Mr – Mr Br –

ELLIE (*rampaging across*). Oh, how wonderful, what a wonderful, clever boy! (*Clutches* HOLLY *to her.*) But please – please, you will have some tea with us, you will have a cuppa and some cake – but no Sachertorte, I'm sorry, no Sachertorte left, we have finished it together, haven't we, Holly, but there is cake – sherry, would you like a glass of sherry?

CELIA. No, no, I won't, thank you very much – um, I've got my tennis, you see. I just wanted to give the news. See you later, darling. (*To* HOLLY.)

ELLIE *accompanies* CELIA *out.*

ELLIE (*off*). Such a boy, such a boy you've got. And such a little gentleman, such a little English gentleman. How lucky you are.

BROWNLOW. Well then. That means you'll be leaving us for London, doesn't it?

HOLLY. Yes. Well, I mean it's in London, Westminster, so I suppose –

BROWNLOW. A scholarship. To Westminster. In London. How proud you must feel. Are you feeling proud, mio?

HOLLY. Well, I haven't had a chance to think about it yet. What it means.

BROWNLOW. What it means is that you're on your way. The little English gentleman is on his way. Away from all this. (*Sweeps arm contemptuously around room.*) And back to his proper little England. (*Sits down at piano, begins to play and sing 'Rule Britannia' savagely.*)

HOLLY *watches him as* ELLIE *opens door in state of excitement, joins in, makes encouraging signs to* HOLLY. HOLLY *joins in, sings more and more full bodiedly.*

They sing through to end.

ELLIE. Oh, that was so good! So good for the spirit! Such a grand song!

BROWNLOW. Thank you, mutti.

ELLIE. And such a lovely lady, Holliday, dein mutti.

BROWNLOW. She is indeed. Thank you, mutti. (*Nods at her pointedly.*)

ELLIE. Well, I leave you, I leave you. And your clever, clever boy. (*Going out.*)

BROWNLOW *laughs.* HOLLY *laughs.*

There is a pause.

HOLLY. They're talking of coming back some time. In the summer. They say once they're away they'll probably miss it, really. And the beach.

BROWNLOW *looks at him.*

HOLLY. I'm sure they will, Lowly. Honestly. And anyway it's not for three months and so we'll have lots of time.

BROWNLOW. Time for what, mio?

HOLLY (*after a little pause*). Well, to teach me.

BROWNLOW. I should like, if I may, to teach you now. This minute. (*Gets up, moves away from piano.*)

HOLLY *goes to piano, sits facing* BROWNLOW, *stretches out his arms, does his finger exercises.* BROWNLOW *gives a slight nod.* HOLLY *turns around, begins to play a hitherto unheard piece of music. Chopin Etude?*

Lights. Curtain.

ACT TWO

Scene One

A few weeks later. Early evening.

SMITHERS' *sitting room.*

HOLLY *is at the piano.* CELIA *is lying on the sofa, smoking.*

HOLLY *completes passage, gets up quickly, stuffs score into his satchel, goes towards door.*

HOLLY. Bye, Mummy.

CELIA *doesn't answer.*

HOLLY. Mummy? (*Goes over to* CELIA.) What is it this time, going dead again or gone blind again? Mummy, please, I'll be late, what is it?

CELIA (*as if coming out of a trance*). Sorry, darling. I've been away somewhere, I think. A bit of a headache.

HOLLY. Oh. Well, you must take some aspirin.

CELIA (*patting sofa.*) Just give me one of your rubs. Just for a minute.

HOLLY. But, Mummy, I –

CELIA. Just for a minute, darling, please.

HOLLY. He gets very fed up when I'm late. (*Going behind* CELIA, *beginning to massage her neck.*)

CELIA. Well, you can tell him you've been looking after me for once. Or I'll write him a note, if you like.

HOLLY. Oh, Mummy. (*Laughs.*) A note.

CELIA. Mmmm – mmmm – deeper, deeper – oh, you've got such a feel for it. You seem to know my neck like your piano, I suppose. Holly, do you love me?

HOLLY. Oh, Mummy, of course I do. Because you're my –

CELIA. No, no, not that, not the usual. I'm being very, very serious. I just want you to say it and nothing more.

HOLLY. Well, I've said it.

CELIA. Well, say it again. Think about it first and then say it. Holly, do you love me?

HOLLY (*after a little pause*). Yes.

CELIA. You don't know how lucky you are being a boy. Look at me – I may not be stupid but I'm almost completely uneducated, really. You're far more educated than I am already. And when you grow up you'll have your freedom, you'll be able to make all kinds of choices. Be what you want. But what am I good for? I can't do anything except what I do. And sometimes that just seems to be nothing. Nothing at all.

HOLLY. But you used to teach girls gym, tennis – and lacrosse.

CELIA. I can scarcely go back to that now, can I? Do you know, I wouldn't even know how to go about getting a job any more.

HOLLY. But you drove ambulances at the air base. You're always saying how much you loved it.

CELIA. Oh, they don't want women driving ambulances now the war's over. They don't need us to be anything except what we've always been now they don't need us for carrying wounded men about.

HOLLY. Mummy, are you crying?

CELIA (*sniffing*). No, not really. Just a little.

HOLLY. But why? Just because you're not educated?

CELIA (*laughs*). Yes, I expect that's it. And because I feel a little sad too, I expect.

HOLLY. But why are you sad?

CELIA. Oh, things, darling, things. Things I wouldn't dream of burdening you with. You wouldn't understand and I don't want you to.

HOLLY. What things?

CELIA. Grown up things, darling. Which are just childish things, really, that happen after a certain age.

Sound of front door opening and closing.

CELIA. Oh, there's your father. Early. So he'll be going out again this evening, won't he?

HOLLY *has gone to pick up his satchel.*

CHARLES *enters.*

CHARLES. Oh, hello, darling. (*Sees* HOLLY.) Off already?

HOLLY. Daddy?

CHARLES. Well, it seems that every time I come in you're going out. Rather like a French farce. At least we've both got our trousers on, eh? (*Laughs.*)

HOLLY (*laughs*). I've got my piano.

CHARLES. Well yes, I assume that. It's been virtually every evening, hasn't it?

HOLLY. He's teaching me some preludes – Chopin – and they're rather difficult.

CHARLES. And you want to master them, do you?

HOLLY. Yes, Daddy.

CHARLES. Well, now your scholarship's in the bag I suppose your time's your own for a bit. After all you've earned it. Earned your Chopin. So. Off you go then.

HOLLY. Thanks, Daddy.

CHARLES (*slightly surprised*). Not at all, Holly.

As HOLLY *goes to door.*

CHARLES. Oh, Holly, there is one thing. You might ask your Mr – Mr – um – no, it's all right, it doesn't matter.

HOLLY *goes out.*

CHARLES. I was going to ask him to find out when I can expect a bill at last. I know he said he wouldn't charge me for the extra hours but I don't feel right about it. It's all a bit awkward if you ask me. Still, mustn't complain, I expect his London tinkler will want it in cash and on the dot – but there's something about him, Mr – Mr – why can we never remember his name?

CELIA. You're going out again, I take it.

CHARLES. A little girl just come in, four years old. We're all hoping to God it isn't polio that did for her, though from what Greatorix says – (*Looks at* CELIA.) Are you all right?

CELIA. A slight headache, that's all.

CHARLES. Have you taken an aspirin?

CELIA. Yes, I took two.

CHARLES. When?

CELIA. About an hour ago.

CHARLES. And you've still got it?

CELIA. Yes, I've just said.

CHARLES. Poor Ceci, poor Ceci. (*Kisses her forehead, goes behind her.*) Here, let's see what I can do. (*Begins to massage her neck.*) You feeling it?

CELIA. Yes. It's making it worse. (*Walks around room, her hand to her head.*)

CHARLES. Oh. Sorry. (*Little pause.*) Shall I get us a drink?

CELIA *nods.*

CHARLES *goes and pours drinks, glancing anxiously at* CELIA, *who lights a cigarette.* CHARLES *goes over, hands her a glass.*

CHARLES. There we are. (*Smiling.*) May I? (*Makes to take cigarette from between* CELIA's *lips.*)

CELIA *moves cigarette away.*

CHARLES. Darling – (*Stops.*) Oh, isn't it your period about now, old girl?

CELIA. Don't you know?

CHARLES. Well, not the precise date, how could I?

CELIA. So you're guessing. Because I've got a headache and I'm feeling low and miserable, it must be old girl's period.

CHARLES. Well, if it's not, then what is it?

CELIA. I suppose people can feel low and miserable because they're actually low and miserable, even if they are women, wives and mothers and aren't allowed to be low and miserable, except when they've got their periods.

CHARLES. Is it the island again? The gang getting you down? (*Little pause.*) Has Moira said something?

CELIA. What sort of something?

CHARLES. Well, the sort of something she's always saying that upsets you.

CELIA. No, Moira hasn't said anything she's always saying that upsets me.

CHARLES. Well, anybody else in the gang? I know how much you hate them but, darling, we're away from here soon – a new life. There'll be a new life.

CELIA. Yes. A new life. A new life. (*Walking about, smoking. Laughs.*) But there's no getting away from the old life, is there? Ever?

CHARLES. No, I suppose not. But the old life merges into the new life and things change directions and – I don't quite know what you mean, Ceci.

CELIA. I'm trying to talk about the old, old life, not this that will be the old life when we get to London, but the old life that was before we came to the island. Do you remember?

CHARLES. Yes, of course I remember. Well, there was quite a lot of it, wasn't there, quite a lot of life before we came here. There was the war, for example. (*Little laugh.*) I mean, which part of the old life?

CELIA. Well, there were certain special moments, I suppose, even in the war, special moments for us – there must have been, mustn't there?

CHARLES. Yes. Yes, quite a few of them. Which ones are you thinking of? I mean, darling, what are you talking about really?

CELIA. Well, Whitstaple. I think I must be talking about Whitstaple.

CHARLES. Whitstaple?

CELIA. Yes. Do you remember us in Whitstaple?

CHARLES. Yes, of course I remember.

CELIA. We went there for the oysters.

CHARLES. Well, darling – yes, the oysters – but we went there to become lovers. Surely that's what you remember about Whitstaple.

CELIA. Yes, yes. All that embarrassment over getting the room for the night.

CHARLES. Rooms actually. We had to take a room each because of that ghastly little landlady – she knew perfectly well what we were up to – so all my shuffling up and down the stairs in the dark. (*Laughing reminiscently.*)

CELIA. Yes, that's how it began. You shuffling about in the dark, me waiting for you in that horrid room with the curtains that didn't close and the window you couldn't open.

CHARLES (*laughs*). Yes, well, I suppose quite a lot of couples got off like that. It was all we could get of romance.

CELIA. Yes, quite a lot of us. Quite a lot of others must have got off like that. Got off on the wrong foot. Deceiving people right from the beginning. Whatever we pretended to each other we knew it was furtive and it was wrong.

CHARLES. Furtive – wrong? It was just how we had to go about things before – before we were properly married. As far as society was concerned, our parents and – for form's sake. Discreet, we were being, that's all.

CELIA. But still, we were different, you and I. We wanted to be different from the others. And that's why we kept saying that whatever happened in our lives together we would always be straight with each other, at least. That was to be our rule. Unbreakable. That we would be straight with each other. We made that rule the very next morning. In Whitstaple.

CHARLES. Well – yes. And we always have been.

CELIA *shakes her head.*

CHARLES. What? What do you mean?

CELIA. Oh, Chaps, not me. I haven't been straight. I haven't been straight with you, Chaps.

CHARLES *stares at her.*

CELIA. I had an affair, you see, Chaps.

CHARLES. An affair? In Whitstaple? We were only there for three days!

CELIA. Oh, don't be so stupid, Charles! Of course not in Whitstaple. Afterwards. After we'd just got married. At the base.

CHARLES (*after a pause*). Who? Who may I ask?

CELIA. It was Johnny.

CHARLES. Johnny? You don't mean Johnny Miller!

CELIA. No, not Johnny Miller.

CHARLES. Which Johnny then, there were several Johnnies, I seem to remember.

CELIA. Johnny Seafield.

CHARLES. Seafield. (*Thinks.*) Johnny Seafield! The one who used to tinkle the piano and lead the sing-songs in the mess?

CELIA. That's right. Piano Johnny we used to call him.

CHARLES. That's not what some of us called him, some of us called him *Pansy* Johnny – and worse.

CELIA. Oh yes, I know you did. That was part of the – well, the joke, really. You thought he was like that because he was boyish and delicate and had a gentle manner.

CHARLES. He was effeminate and – and he had a kind of lisp. He made our skins crawl.

CELIA (*laughs*). You were such stupid chaps. Blind, the lot of you. We women knew what he was really like. And he was brave. Brave and doomed.

CHARLES. They were all brave, and a lot of them doomed. He wasn't the only one to buy it, you know.

CELIA. I know. Oh, how I know. He and Julian Lownes and Dickie Storbuck. All in the same afternoon.

CHARLES. But it was him you had a fling with, was it? Or did you have a fling with all of them? All three?

CELIA *gives him a look.*

CELIA. It wasn't a fling. It was a sadness. The saddest time in my life. I used to watch the skies for him and when I saw him coming back I'd think, well, that's one more time, one more time at least, God has given us.

CHARLES. One more time God had given you – *God* had given you – for you and he to – to – where did you do it?

CELIA. Rose House.

CHARLES. Rose House. But that was the vicarage! You did it in the vicarage!

CELIA. The vicar was Johnny's uncle. He was the only person who knew. And he understood. Understood everything. Sometimes he stood with me watching the skies. Both of us looking for Johnny's plane.

CHARLES. Well, we watched the skies too, wondering who was coming back – how many we could patch up – how many we could send up again, knowing that the more often we sent them back, the more likely it was – and that went for your Johnny too. For all the Johnnies we had to put back in the skies. Pansies or not.

CELIA. It wasn't your fault.

CHARLES. What do you mean it wasn't my fault, of course it wasn't my fault that you and your Johnny –

CELIA. No, no, I meant it wasn't your fault that you weren't up in the skies with them. You did the only job you could do. Just as I did in the ambulances.

CHARLES. Are you saying I should be ashamed? That while you were having your – your – with him up in the skies – I should be ashamed for being down there on the ground?

CELIA. No, I'm saying you shouldn't be. That's it, you see, that's what I'm trying to explain. You and I – well, we had a chance and a future. For us, we could hope it would be over one day, there'd be peace and our lives to live. But Johnny – and the others too, of course – didn't have that hope –

CHARLES. Look – (*Getting up.*) I know – I know what sort of thing went on. I'd supposed you were exempt from all that panic and living-in-the-moment stuff. But if you weren't – well, God knows how many stories there are to tell that shouldn't be told – what on earth is the bloody point –

CELIA. Of being straight you mean? When we promised we would be. That was our rule.

CHARLES. Well, it's a bit late, isn't it? A dozen years or so late.

CELIA. I couldn't have told you then, not while it was going on – and I couldn't have told you afterwards – after he'd gone. It would have been unfair on Johnny – to my memory of him – if he'd been the cause for unhappiness between us.

CHARLES. Well then, why now? Why now when he's been at the bottom of the sea for seven or eight years and it no longer matters? You don't have to be straight when it no longer matters, there's no point to it. No – no moral value even. I mean – I mean, for God's sake, woman, I come home from a day's work, this morning's post mortems behind me, and tomorrow's – no, tonight's probably – a child of four – a little girl of four and it could be polio, here on this island – if so, God help all of us who have children – looking forward – just looking forward to being alone with you, having our usual drink, our usual – our usual – and this. I get this. Why?

CELIA. But you see, Chaps, you see, you talked about a new life in London and I'm afraid, you see. So afraid.

CHARLES. Of London? But you've been begging to go to London! Everything I've done has been to get you to London! We're only going there because of you.

CELIA. But what I'm afraid of, Chaps – my dear old Chaps – is that it won't be a new life. Because we'll be taking our old life with us, you see.

CHARLES. Taking what you've told me with us, you mean? So why did you tell me? Because if I didn't know there'd be nothing to take with us, would there?

CELIA *looks at him.*

CHARLES. What?

CELIA. There's Holly to take with us.

CHARLES. Holly? What do you mean?

There is a pause.

CHARLES. That's not true.

CELIA. He'll have to know. One day. One day soon. We've got to be straight with him. Or at least I've got to be. He can't grow up in a lie and find out somehow, people always do, and that would be the worst. Going on lying to him, going on pretending – (*Shakes her head.*) we've got to be straight.

CHARLES *has gone over, poured himself another drink.*

CHARLES. Everything's upside down. Just some minutes ago it was right side up and now it's upside down. Everything. (*Sinks into sofa.*) I never thought the day would come when

I'd – when I'd hate you. Have you any idea what you've
done? Do you realise what it'll be like from now on for me
to be me? How I'll look at you and him? How I'll think of
you and him? Every time I look at you and him together I'll
see you at Rose House and I'll see him at Rose House and
I'll see that pansy at Rose House, the three of you at Rose
House – how can I hope to go on?

CELIA. Oh, you foolish man, how can Holly be anything else
but yours? I wanted to enjoy this, I really wanted to, I
wanted to let you stew away, I was looking forward to it. I
think I deserved that. And so did you. But the awful truth is
I love you and I can't get away from that so I can't bear to
see you hurt.

CHARLES. You mean – you mean this is a joke? Is it a joke?
Is that what it is? One of your stupid games, like pretending
you've gone blind or that you're in a coma or are having a
stroke, one of your dramatising, one of your attention-
seeking silly games? Can it really be? Something like this –
something as dangerous as this? God damn you, Ceci, God
damn you!

CELIA. I have a right! Because I wanted you to feel what I've
been feeling. It was my revenge.

CHARLES. Revenge? Revenge for what?

CELIA. Moira, damn you! Moira, Moira, Moira!

CHARLES. Moira? What has Moira got to do with any of this?

CELIA. You might as well be straight, Charles. She told me
herself, you see.

CHARLES (*after a long pause*). She told you.

CELIA. And how many others have there been?

CHARLES. Never anyone. Only her. I swear, darling.

CELIA. Why should I believe you?

CHARLES. Because you know me.

CELIA. No, I don't know you. We don't know each other,
that's what we're discovering.

CHARLES. You do know me, Ceci. Everything about me that matters. The whole me. You're the only person in the world who knows the whole of me.

CELIA. I know the whole of you has been unfaithful – lied to me – betrayed me – and with my best friend.

CHARLES. Oh, now, darling, your best friend? You can't stand her.

CELIA. She's still my best friend on this bloody island anyway. My only friend. Well. Are you going to tell me what happened and how it wasn't your fault really?

CHARLES. Of course it was my fault. I accept that completely. Though it wasn't entirely my fault. I mean – I mean – look, darling, what happened was that she 'phoned me. At the hospital. She needed my professional advice.

CELIA. Your professional advice? Why? Was she dead?

CHARLES. It was about Richard. She wanted to talk to me about something that was wrong with Richard. And she asked me not to mention it to anyone. Not even you.

CELIA. Ahah.

CHARLES. So I looked in on the way back –

CELIA. And when was this?

CHARLES. I don't know – about two months ago it must have been, I suppose.

CELIA. Two months. Go on.

CHARLES. I looked in on the way back and she gave me a cup of tea.

There is a long pause.

CELIA (*helpfully*). She gave you a cup of tea.

CHARLES. Well – then she told me about Richard.

CELIA. What did she tell you?

CHARLES. Well, actually, darling, it's still – well, confidential. A matter of professional etiquette.

CELIA. Oh, I see. And it doesn't matter that she goes about blabbing about you and her because she hasn't any professional etiquette to worry about, has she?

CHARLES. He's impotent.

CELIA. Oh, dear. Poor Moira. So you were called in as a replacement?

CHARLES (*in spite of himself, lets out a little bark of laughter. After a pause*). He absolutely refuses to discuss it with her so she wondered whether I could find some way to – to help him.

CELIA. And how had you planned to do it? Go up to him and say, 'Oh, Richard, old boy, I was rogering Moira the other afternoon and she happened to mention that you're having a little problem, so perhaps you'd like to pop in home and watch me when I'm at it.'

CHARLES. You say you want to find out what happened but you won't let me tell you, tell you properly.

CELIA. Oh, I'm so sorry. Do go on. Please.

CHARLES. Well, it seems things are pretty bad between them. In every possible way, really. Richard's not making out too well in his new job – well, like the rest of us he was out of things for nearly five years and now there are much younger chaps coming into insurance straight from the National Service and universities – so he feels lost. Afraid of getting the sack, drinking far too much and – and – well, taking it out on Moira and sometimes quite violently. You see. Then she has to put on this front for the rest of the world – you know how she is, always cheerful and laughing – and suddenly there she was, breaking down in front of me. And I put my arms around her and she seemed to assume – and I didn't know how to refuse. Yes, that's what it comes down to. I was frightened of hurting her. You see, Ceci? I know it sounds feeble but that's what really happened.

CELIA. Where did you do it, by the way?

CHARLES. Why?

CELIA. In their bedroom, was it?

CHARLES (*indignantly*). Of course not.

CELIA. Where then, darling? On the floor – on the sofa, perhaps?

CHARLES. In the spare room. Spare bedroom.

CELIA. Oh, I don't think so, darling. I've seen that spare room, it hasn't even got a bed, it's got a cot, it wouldn't support Moira on her own, let alone the two of you. I should think you had to do it in their bedroom.

CHARLES. It was in the spare room –

CELIA. And did you enjoy it, darling? Because that's the main thing, isn't it?

CHARLES. Celia, really!

CELIA. Oh, don't be such a prude, Charles. You can tell your wife, surely?

CHARLES. I don't know – I don't know – I did it because it seemed the right thing to do – that's what I'm trying to explain – even though I knew it was the wrong thing, at that moment – at that particular moment it seemed – (*Gestures.*) the right thing. I don't think I was trying to enjoy it, I was just trying to – to do it.

CELIA. And the other times?

CHARLES *shrugs.*

CELIA. How many other times have there been?

CHARLES. Five, I think. Yes, five.

CELIA. And how did you manage them, your little visits? Oh, of course! When you have to go out in the evenings. To the hospital. To visit your corpses. For their post mortems that you hate doing, poor lamb.

There is a pause.

CHARLES. Needless to say, there won't be any more – any more –

CELIA. So you'll be keeping the little polio girl for the morning after all, will you? Really, Charles, how sickening. (*There is a pause.*) But of course, in London, where there will be lots and lots of fat little Moiras laughing and cheerful with impotent husbands, it'll be so much easier for you. You won't even have to lie to me.

CHARLES. Damn Moira – why did she have to tell you, why? I simply don't understand.

CELIA. She didn't have to tell me. She just couldn't help herself. After tennis the other day she suddenly started on Richard. She said she's fairly sure he has a floozy in London and that's why he'd lost interest in her and why he was drinking. And I said – I said – hah! (*Laughs.*) I said, '*Fairly* sure? But you must know. I mean, I'd *always* know if Charles had been with another woman – *fairly* sure wouldn't come into it. I'd just *know*. Just by looking at him.' And she said, 'Oh, how close you and Charles must be if you'd know about him just like that. That's what I call a real marriage, darling.' And I caught her look – a little gleam in her eye, a sort of grin in her eye. That's how she told me. The grin in her eye. I didn't know anything about it from you, however often I'd looked at you. Even now I wouldn't know anything about it just from looking at you. (*Pause.*) I could have had an affair with Johnny. He wanted me to. And I was so – so proud of myself for not. Because I was attracted to him. Very attracted. But then I could never do anything like that to you, could I? I couldn't stand the pain of the pain I'd be giving you – knowing you as I do. But now – what difference would it have made? None at all. Except to me of course. (*Smiles at him.*)

CHARLES (*attempts to smile back*). Everything's going to be all right. I'll make sure. (*Puts a hand out towards her.*)

CELIA *looks at him in sudden horrified bewilderment.*

CELIA. But I don't believe you. It's true – I've never known you. Never really known you. So how can I live with you any more – in London or anywhere? (*Little pause.*) I'm not going to be like all those others. You've been like those other men but I'm not going to be like their women –

standing by my man when I don't know what man I'm standing by. No, Charles, I've got to leave. I've got to take Holly and leave. Even though I've got nowhere to go because you've left me with nothing – there's nothing for me, nothing I can do in life, nowhere to go. But I'd rather nothing than be with you, just another man I don't know and can't trust. (*Gets up, goes towards door, collapses, sobbing.*) Oh, mama, mama, help me, help me – oh – oh!

CHARLES, *appalled and distressed, goes to her.*

CHARLES. Oh, my Ceci, my poor darling Ceci! What have I done? Oh, please, Ceci, please – (*Attempts to put his arms around her.*)

CELIA (*pushing him away*). No, leave me alone! Leave me alone!

CHARLES. Ceci, Ceci – (*Forces his arms around her, holds her tightly.*)

CELIA *rocks and keens in his arms. Keening fades away. They cling together as if saving themselves. They become aware of a noise off, separate quickly, desperately trying to compose themselves as:*

Door opens. HOLLY *enters, followed by* BROWNLOW.

CELIA. Oh, hello, darling, what are you doing back so soon? (*Seeing* BROWNLOW.) Everything all right?

BROWNLOW. Oh, yes, indeed. It's just that I've had a rather exciting telegram from a friend of mine in London – a conductor. Teddy Schefflen. Apparently they're going to be playing a small piece of mine at his concert on Saturday.

CELIA. Oh, how exciting, eh, darling?

CHARLES. Yes, yes, congratulations.

There is a pause.

CELIA. Would you like a drink?

BROWNLOW. Thank you, if I may. But we mustn't stay long, we haven't begun our lesson yet.

CHARLES. We're drinking gin and tonic. Will that do?

BROWNLOW. Thank you.

CELIA. Do sit down.

BROWNLOW (*sitting down*). I wondered if you'd let Holly come with me. Stay over on Saturday night, coming back on Sunday evening. I think it could be very educative – there are a number of other concerts over the weekend – and I'd make sure of course that he would be well looked after.

CELIA. Well, that sounds – that sounds – what do you think, darling?

CHARLES. Well – here, Holly, give this to Mr – (*Hands HOLLY drink.*)

HOLLY *takes drink over to* BROWNLOW.

BROWNLOW. We studied music together, Teddy and I. And his wife. All three of us. She's a flautist. Now they have a delightful baby, very chubby. Their house is in Fulham – very convenient for the concerts. He's conducting two of them, the one with my piece and another on Sunday morning. He really is becoming something of a maestro, Teddy.

CELIA. It would be awfully good for him, darling. And I mean, as we're going to London, he'll already know something about music halls.

BROWNLOW. We'll be visiting several. Concert halls. Though I'm not so sure about music halls. (*Gives a little laugh.*) Anyway, he'll learn a lot. We'll all conspire to make sure of it.

CELIA. And you'd like that, darling, would you? (*To* HOLLY.)

HOLLY. Oh, yes – yes. Very much.

CHARLES (*making an effort*). But you must let me know about the tickets, the train and any expenses. I insist on that. Insist on it.

CELIA. My husband is very pernickety about things like that, aren't you, darling?

CHARLES. I just don't want Mr – um – anybody to be out of pocket.

BROWNLOW. Oh, I shan't be, I'll make sure of it.

CHARLES. Yes, please do.

There is a pause.

CELIA. How's the cat – Miaow – how's Miaow?

Lights.

Scene Two

The following Sunday. Nine p.m.

BROWNLOW*'s study/sitting room.*

ELLIE *is at the piano, accompanying herself as she sings a Viennese folk song. She plays well, sings well. She is drunk. She concludes song triumphantly and theatrically, drinks from glass on piano.*

Sound of doorbell.

ELLIE (*in German*). What? Who is this now at this hour? Has he forgotten his keys? (*Goes to window, taps on it.*) Thomas? Thomas? Is that you there, Thomas?

Sound of voice off.

ELLIE (*in English*). Who is it? (*Obviously can't hear. In German.*) Oh God, it's the police, it's the police, they've come to take me, come to take us! (*Cowers.*) Thomas, Thomas, why aren't you here?

Doorbell rings again imperiously.

ELLIE *goes out. Voices off.*

CHARLES (*off*). Is my son here?

ELLIE (*off*). Your son, bitte?

CHARLES (*off*). Yes, my son. Holly. Is he here, please?

ELLIE (*off*). Oh, Holly, yes, yes, of course, of course! He's with Thomas.

ELLIE *holds door open.* CHARLES *enters.*

ELLIE (*attempting to conceal drunkenness*). So you're the father, the father of Holly. I'm so sorry, I couldn't see you, I thought it was the police, you see.

CHARLES. The police? (*Anxiously.*) Why did you think I was the police?

ELLIE. Bitte?

CHARLES. Why are you expecting the police?

ELLIE. Oh, no, no, it's just that sometimes when it's late – so. You are the father of our boy.

CHARLES. I'm Holly's father, yes. I thought you said he was here.

ELLIE. Bitte?

CHARLES. My son and your son, isn't it, you said at the door they were here. Didn't you?

ELLIE. Ah yes, well, they were here before – for a long time – and then I went upstairs to rest and I came downstairs and you were at the window, no, you were at the door and – the kitchen, perhaps they are in the kitchen having a cuppa. (*Goes to the door, screams out.*) Thomas – Thomas – Holliday – Holliday, here is your father, are you there, are you there? (*Comes back in.*) No, there is no light, they are not in the kitchen, no. Well, they must have gone out for a walk, yes?

CHARLES. A walk? At this hour?

ELLIE. Can I offer you a drink? It is only sherry but it is new, a fresh bottle.

CHARLES. No, thank you. When did they get back?

ELLIE. Back? Bitte?

CHARLES. When did they get back from London?

ELLIE. Oh, I don't know, let me think – back, back – this afternoon early, I made them some lunch, I remember, yes, soup and corn beef –

CHARLES. But they were meant to be coming back on the last ferry which was two hours ago – we've been getting worried, very worried – and you say they've been here all day virtually? Why didn't he 'phone us at least?

ELLIE. Yes, I know, so silly, I keep telling him he must have a telephone for his asthma but no, he will not –

CHARLES. But why are they back so early?

ELLIE. I think my boy, there was some quarrel with his friend in London – Teddy – sometimes they have terrible arguments – shouting anger, tears, you know with friends. Yes, probably there was a fight, I don't know.

CHARLES. I see. A fight with his friend – Teddy. (*Little pause, thinks.*) But there's a wife, isn't there, and a baby?

ELLIE. Teddy, a wife, baby? (*Laughs.*) No, no. Not for Teddy a wife and a baby.

CHARLES. But your son said – I remember distinctly – a wife, a baby – his friends, a husband, a wife and a baby.

ELLIE. Ah, that is Teddy's sister, Debbie. She has a baby, yes. But not husband. He ran away – poof! And no wife for Teddy.

CHARLES. And what have they been doing here all day?

ELLIE. Doing? Who?

CHARLES. My son and your son, what have they been doing since they got back? (*Just controlling anger.*)

ELLIE. Nothing. Playing like always. Always they play. Like children they are. Except when Holliday is at the piano and my boy is teaching him. Then goodness, my goodness, very serious, very strong. Yes, the music, that is always serious. But he is a genius. One day he will be a great artist, famous everywhere – oh, if I should live to see it, that's all I hope

for! And your boy too, your Holliday – my son, he hates to
teach all the children here – (*In German.*) lumpen fingers –
(*In English.*) he calls them, how you say? Yes, their fingers
are lumps. They have no music in their heads, their bodies,
only English stupidity and nice – all so nice. But his Holly,
him he loves and worships, he has a beautiful gift, a beautiful soul – not English and nice but a free soul like his, dancing, dancing – so they dance together. (*Wagging her head,
crooning.*) Like this, like this, they are, to make you cry.

CHARLES. Really. And you don't know where they are now?

ELLIE. Oh, no. Perhaps on the beach. By the sea. They like to
hear the sea, to inspire them.

CHARLES. Do they. And what sort of games do they play
when they're not at the piano?

ELLIE. Just ordinary games. They pretend – you know –
pretend they are at anger between them, and cruelty – and
then if he cries they are friends again. Like children, you
see. Playing, crying, holding each other – (*Stops. Looks at
CHARLES, suddenly worried.*) You are angry. Oh, please
do not be angry, do not be English – be nice, not like
English nice, there must be no trouble, no more trouble – it
is not his fault if he loves to teach, people do not understand
– we cannot move away, oh, we cannot move away again –
please, Mr Holly's father, please be kind. (*Begins to cry,
sags into a chair. In German.*) Oh, what have I said, what
have I done?

CHARLES *stares at her in disgust.*

Door opens. BROWNLOW *enters.*

CHARLES. What have you done with my son?

BROWNLOW. I've just taken him home. To your home. Your
wife told me you'd come over here so I hurried back.

CHARLES. He's been here all afternoon, I gather.

BROWNLOW. Yes, well, we came back early – the lunch time
concert was cancelled – and as I knew you weren't
expecting him back until the last ferry –

CHARLES. The last ferry is at six o'clock on Sundays.

BROWNLOW. Oh, is it? I assumed it was the same time as in the week. I'm very sorry – but even so we're only an hour or so later than –

CHARLES. That's not the point.

BROWNLOW. What is the point?

CHARLES. The point is – the point is that I've been talking to your mother. I think I have a fairly good idea – no, I won't call it a good idea – but an idea of the sort of thing that's been going on between you and my son.

BROWNLOW. Indeed? What has been going on between your son and myself, may I ask? What is this idea you have of what has been going on?

CHARLES. Let's just say that you are to have nothing further to do with him. Do you understand me?

BROWNLOW. No – no, I don't understand. I've done nothing wrong. We did nothing wrong together. I would never do anything to harm your son. Never. So please, please don't stop his lessons – he will never find another teacher who understands him as I do, who knows his talents –

CHARLES. If I catch you anywhere near him I'll go to the police.

ELLIE (*in German*). The police, the police – there, I warned you!

BROWNLOW. I don't care – go to the police, I'm not frightened, I'm not ashamed, I have nothing to be ashamed of.

CHARLES. Yes, you probably believe that, that's just it, isn't it, with a type like you. You don't know what decency is, you have no idea, no sense, no understanding even of what it is to be straight. You filthy, little – Jew.

ELLIE. No, no, we are not Jews! Not Jews!

CHARLES *turns, goes out.*

ELLIE (*in German*). See? See what you've done? He'll go to the police and we'll be finished.

BROWNLOW. What did you say to him? What did you tell him about me – about Holly and me?

ELLIE (*in German*). Nothing – nothing – I said how good you were to each other, how happy, how you taught him and sometimes that you were strict, that you loved each other like children –

BROWNLOW. Loved each other – loved each other like children – (*Sinks into a chair, puts his face into his hands, his shoulders begin to shake.*)

ELLIE *goes over to him, kneels beside him, strokes his head.*

ELLIE (*in German*). There, there, Thomas, my poor, poor Thomas. (*Puts her arms around him, begins to rock him. He rocks with her.*)

Lights.

Scene Three

The same.

SMITHERS' *sitting room.*

HOLLY'*s overnight bag by sofa.* HOLLY *is sitting at piano stool, facing away from piano, drinking cup of tea.*

CELIA *is lying on sofa, smoking.*

CELIA. I must say, darling, it does sound all terribly Bohemian and hothousey. And what was it about, this ferocious row?

HOLLY. Oh, a bit of music – well, that's what started it anyway, I couldn't follow the rest of it, it was all about people I don't know, but it was the Berg that did it in the first place.

CELIA. The Berg? What Berg?

HOLLY. The composer, Alban Berg. They were trying to remember the first bars of some piano piece, I don't know which one, but they had a bet on it, you see – well, what happened was that Teddy began to play it and Lowly –

CELIA. Who?

HOLLY. Mr Brownlow, that's what everybody calls him in London, Lowly. Anyway, he, Mr Brownlow, said that Teddy had got it wrong and it started like this and he showed him, and then they had their bet and then Teddy couldn't find the music and Mr Brownlow said he was hiding it because he knew he'd lost the bet and – and so, you know, that's when it went all over the place.

CELIA. But, poor darling, how embarrassing for you. What on earth did you do?

HOLLY. Oh, I just went back to our room.

CELIA. Our room? Whose room?

HOLLY. Well, the bedroom.

CELIA. Oh. So you and Mr Brownlow shared a bedroom, did you?

HOLLY. Oh no, not really, I was on a sofa thing in the hall but I left my stuff in the room he was sleeping in so I went there and got the score for the lunch time concert they'd given me.

CELIA. Then Teddy threw you both out, did he?

HOLLY. No, no, he didn't throw us out, Mummy. It was all quite friendly after that, except it turned out the concert had been cancelled or something so he, Mr Brownlow, said let's go back and enjoy the weather and we said good-bye. It was all friendly and as if nothing had happened really.

CELIA. Well, I suppose musicians and people like that tend to have tantrums and melodramas. It's probably all quite fun in a way. And what was the little wife and baby doing during all this?

HOLLY. Oh, she didn't pay much attention, as if she were quite used to it.

CELIA. Even so, you should have been more thoughtful,
    darling. He probably doesn't think about parental worries
    and fears when children are late – trains do crash, ferries do
    sink – so you should have popped in to let us know you
    were safe at least.

HOLLY. Well, he didn't think you'd expect us back, he
    explained to you, Mummy, he just got the time wrong for
    Sundays, that's all.

CELIA. Well, the next time (*Yawns.*) you'll know what to do.
    Your father really was getting into quite a state.

HOLLY. Well, I'm sorry. Do you mind if I just play
    something? It was in the concert last night and we've been
    practising playing it from memory this afternoon but I'm
    afraid it'll slip away if I don't do it once more before I go –
    (*Notices that* CELIA *isn't paying attention, turns to piano,
    begins to play thoughtfully.*)

    CELIA *goes on smoking,* HOLLY *goes on playing.*

    CELIA, *suddenly becoming aware of* HOLLY, *looks at him.
    She stubs out cigarette, looks at* HOLLY *again.*

CELIA (*sternly*). Holly, come here.

    HOLLY *goes on playing, as if unaware.*

CELIA (*more loudly and sternly*). Holly. I said come here.
    This minute.

    HOLLY *sighs, gets up, goes over.*

HOLLY. What, Mummy, I was just –

CELIA. Sit down.

HOLLY (*going to sit down*). I was just getting to the bit I
    wanted to –

CELIA. Not there. Here. (*Pats side of sofa.*)

    HOLLY *sits on sofa.*

CELIA. Now, look at me. Straight in the eye, my boy. I want
    the truth.

    There is a long pause.

HOLLY. Well about what, Mummy?

CELIA. You know what about. (*Pause.*) Do you love me?

HOLLY. Oh, honestly, Mummy.

CELIA. I want an answer.

HOLLY. Of course I do. You know I do.

CELIA. Why? Tell me why.

HOLLY. Well, because you're my mother.

CELIA. That's not good enough.

HOLLY. Why not?

CELIA. Because I'm not your mother. You're adopted. There. What do you say to that?

HOLLY stands, trembling and swaying, as if in shock.

CELIA (*suddenly alarmed*). Darling – darling!

HOLLY (*holds up his hand*). Mummy, I think that's the most terrific news I've ever heard. I always knew it – well, I always hoped it anyway. Thank you, Mummy.

CELIA grabs him, begins to tickle him. HOLLY squirms, giggling helplessly, pulls himself away.

HOLLY. Now I've got to get back –

CELIA. Twiddle my toes. Twiddle my toes first, go on. They feel stiff and crampy. Just for two minutes.

HOLLY. Ohh. Two minutes. Exactly two minutes. (*Looks at his watch, sits down.*)

Sound of front door opening, closing.

CELIA. Ah, there's your father.

CHARLES enters, taking in HOLLY massaging CELIA's toes.

CELIA. Oh, there you are, darling, and here he is, as I expect you already know.

HOLLY (*gets up*). Hello, Daddy.

CELIA. Darling, what is it?

CHARLES. Holly, sit down, please.

HOLLY *sits down.*

CELIA. What is it, Charles?

CHARLES. I've just been speaking to that creature.

CELIA. What creature?

CHARLES. That creature and his mother. I know what sort of thing's been going on. What I don't know is exactly how far it went. (*Little pause.*) Holly?

CELIA. Charles, shouldn't we –

CHARLES. Holly.

HOLLY. I – I don't know what you mean, Daddy.

CHARLES. I think you do. When you 'played' together, for instance.

HOLLY. We just played Beethoven – Chopin –

CHARLES. No, not when you played together on the piano. When you 'played' together like children. What did you do then, when you 'played' together like children?

HOLLY. He – he – sometimes he pretended to get cross – that's all – when I went wrong on the piano. And – and it was just a game. He didn't mean anything. I didn't mind. It's just – just his way of teaching me, to make it more – to make me concentrate more.

CHARLES. And your dancing together, was that to make you concentrate more?

HOLLY. Dancing?

CHARLES. Dancing.

HOLLY. Well, we didn't – I mean – there's a bit of Handel he used to play and he taught me a few steps –

CHARLES. Show me.

CELIA. Charles.

CHARLES. Show me, please, Holly.

HOLLY, *after a pause, takes a few steps, a pirouette, then a few more steps, bows.*

CHARLES. So he played and you did that for him. (*Little pause.*) When you were in London with his friend – Teddy – what then?

CELIA. There was Teddy's wife and the baby.

CHARLES. In London with his friend, Teddy, and Teddy's sister and her baby by someone who's left her, what then?

There is a pause.

CHARLES. What did you do, you and Mr – (*Gestures.*) your dancing master. What did you do together in London?

HOLLY. Nothing. We went to a concert in the evening and a walk and then there was a quarrel over music and then the concert was cancelled and then we came back and we didn't know you were waiting for us and – and that's all.

CHARLES. And what were the sleeping arrangements?

HOLLY. Well, I slept in the room with the baby.

CELIA. Yes, he was just telling me about it, Charles.

CHARLES. You and the baby?

HOLLY. Yes. And then the baby woke up and the mother came in and I slept in the hall on the sofa.

There is a pause.

CHARLES. I told your friend that he's not to see you again. You will stay away from him, Holly. Is that understood?

HOLLY *nods.*

CHARLES. Good. If I had my way I'd drive him off the island. There's nothing I'd like better. But as we're leaving ourselves, it would probably just cause a lot of fuss and we don't want the fuss following us to London like a plague, and there'd be bound to be talk about you, what you let happen to you –

CELIA. Darling!

CHARLES. You know this island, for God's sakes, better than anyone. Whatever the truth, there'd be gossip.

CELIA (*turns to* HOLLY). All Daddy's saying is that people are so silly and nasty and quick to make silly and nasty things up – that you should – should, well, keep mum.

CHARLES (*as if ignoring her*). The point is you're starting your scholarship with a clean sheet as far as everybody else knows, you'll just have to make sure you keep it that way. Now we won't discuss this any more ever again. All right, Holly?

HOLLY *doesn't reply.*

CHARLES. Now off you go.

HOLLY. Where, Daddy?

CHARLES. To bed of course.

CELIA. Yes, darling, you should, you've had a – a long day – a nice hot bath and then tomorrow everything will be back to normal.

HOLLY. But he didn't do anything wrong. He was always very nice – kind – kind to me. Honestly.

CHARLES. I told you, we're not going to talk about this any more. And I told you to go to bed.

HOLLY *sits for a moment, as if to speak, then gets up, goes to door, turns defiantly to the piano, sits down, begins to play a brief melange out of which 'Rule Britannia' emerges.*

CHARLES, *after a moment, gets up, goes to* HOLLY.

CHARLES. Go to bed, I say. Go to bed!

HOLLY *continues playing.* CHARLES *makes as if to strike him.*

CELIA. Charles!

CHARLES *just controls himself, looks from* HOLLY *to* CELIA, *goes to door, turns.*

CHARLES. Pansy Johnny's boy. That's who you are. Pansy Johnny's boy. (*Goes out.*)

HOLLY *continues playing, stops.*

HOLLY. What did he mean, Pansy Johnny's boy?

CELIA (*gets up, goes to him*). Nothing really, darling. Just a grown up sort of thing. One day you'll find out all about it, I expect. But there's no rush. (*Puts a hand on his head, looks towards door, goes out.*)

HOLLY *sits for a moment, then turns to piano, continues playing 'Rule Britannia.'*

Lights going down as lights coming up on BROWNLOW's *study,* HOLLY *still playing:*

Scene Four

The present. A few minutes after Act One, Scene One.

BROWNLOW's *study/sitting room.*

HOLLY *is sitting in armchair, smoking, bowl as ashtray cupped in his hand.*

BROWNLOW *enters, carrying tray on which decanter and two glasses.*

BROWNLOW. And when are you planning to go back? To Australia, I mean, Melbourne?

HOLLY. Oh, when I've cleared up a few things, settled a few things.

BROWNLOW *has put tray on table. Picks up decanter, holds it up, inspects it.*

BROWNLOW. I can't see any sediment, rather a lovely colour, what would one call it? Tawny? No, no, of course not, that's for port, isn't it? Topaz, what about topaz? Oh yes, there are one or two black spots floating around, I must try and keep them out of your glass. (*Pours sherry into a glass, brings it over to* HOLLY, *puts it beside him. Gives a little cough.*)

HOLLY. Oh, I'm smoking, I'm sorry, I forgot.

BROWNLOW (*stepping away*). No, no, that's all right. As long as I keep my distance. (*Pouring himself a glass of sherry.*) So much dust in the room anyway, in the corners, I'm always telling Mrs Jameson to get into the corners but I don't think she ever does. There. (*Sitting down at table.*) I'm quite safe over here.

HOLLY (*indicating bowl*). Is it all right to use this as an ashtray?

BROWNLOW. Oh, yes, yes, indeed.

HOLLY. It's pretty. (*Looking at bowl properly.*)

BROWNLOW. Yes, very useful, for little odds and ends. My mother used to have it by her bed. For her teeth actually.

HOLLY *puts bowl down beside him.*

BROWNLOW. And your parents, how are they, are they still with us?

HOLLY. Not my mother. She died fifteen, no, sixteen years ago. Cancer.

BROWNLOW. Oh, I'm so sorry. She always seemed so – so vivid to me.

HOLLY. Yes, she seemed vivid to quite a few people. Perhaps still does. I hope so, anyway.

BROWNLOW. But your father, he's well, is he?

HOLLY. Oh, yes. He's retired of course. Lives on the Isle of Wight with his second wife and their two children.

BROWNLOW. The Isle of Wight? That's – that's convenient. Now that you're here, you can just pop across –

HOLLY. Yes, but I doubt if I'll have the time.

BROWNLOW. But you found time for me.

HOLLY. Yes. Yes, I did.

Pause.

BROWNLOW. So. Life – life, um – and you? What has become of you, may I ask?

HOLLY. I'm a doctor.

BROWNLOW. Ah. And are you also a pathologist like your father?

HOLLY. No, I'm a psychiatrist.

BROWNLOW. A psychiatrist? Ah. So you abandoned your music then, after all?

HOLLY. No. No, I think it abandoned me. My daughter has a gift, something of a gift. She's only ten but her mother keeps her at it. She's a professional cellist – my wife, that is.

BROWNLOW. Oh. So it's the cello for your daughter, not the piano.

HOLLY. The violin actually. But her brother likes to play the piano when he's in the mood and can't find anything better to do.

BROWNLOW. Well, it sounds a happy life. And a complete life. A happy and complete life that you've made for yourself in Australia.

HOLLY. Yes, I suppose it does sound that. Though one never knows, does one, almost from minute to minute, what lies ahead – what memories lie ahead, even. Or don't lie ahead, as it turns out. Like the music. The music that won't come back.

BROWNLOW. I'm sorry?

HOLLY. I think I mentioned it before you got the sherry. Which is actually remarkably drinkable, by the way. It was a bagatelle.

BROWNLOW. A bagatelle, was it?

HOLLY. Yes. You wrote it especially for me. 'A Bagatelle for Mio' you called it. It was played on Radio 3. The Third programme, I mean. Ring any bells?

BROWNLOW. No, it doesn't, I'm afraid. But it was a very long time ago, wasn't it? Some thirty years.

HOLLY. But might you still have the score somewhere?

BROWNLOW. No, I've thrown everything out from those days.

HOLLY. Oh. But could it still be in you, lurking – waiting to come out again? Perhaps if you tried on the keys for a few minutes, see if anything bobs up? I'll recognise it from just a few notes, I know I will. (*Little pause.*) Would you mind? Um, giving it a go? On the keys?

BROWNLOW *gets up, goes across to piano, sits on stool, puts his hands out as if to play. Turns.*

BROWNLOW. I'd rather not. I'd really rather not. There hasn't been music for years – no concertos, no bagatelles, not even dreams of concertos, not even memories of bagatelles – nothing, for years and years. So why have you come here? You come looking me up like this, from so long ago, out of the blue, out of the darkness, remembering this, trying to make me remember that – what do you want? What do you want? To punish? To forgive? (*Laughs.*) It's too late – far too late – (*Begins to wheeze, gropes for inhaler in his pocket, drops it to the floor.*)

HOLLY, *after a moment, comes over, picks up inhaler, puts an arm around* BROWNLOW, *supports him, puts inhaler in his hand, helps him to apply it. Steps away.* BROWNLOW *begins to recover.*

HOLLY. Are you all right?

BROWNLOW *nods.*

HOLLY. I'm so sorry. I just wanted to remember the Bagatelle. You see, I remember everything else as clearly as I want to, I really do. But the Bagatelle, not remembering it has been driving me mad. I shouldn't have been so pressing, I'm sorry. Though oddly enough – for what it's worth – I think (*Hums.*) – isn't that it?

BROWNLOW *shakes his head.*

HOLLY. No, it isn't, is it? Oh well, it'll just have to nag away at me until I forget to try to remember it. (*Hums again, shakes his head.*) No. (*Laughs.*)

BROWNLOW *laughs.*

HOLLY (*looks at his watch*). Good heavens, I'd better be on my way. Leave you in peace. Here – (*Holds out his hand. BROWNLOW takes it.*) There, you see. Still real, I hope.

BROWNLOW (*clutching HOLLY's hand*). No, stay. Stay and talk a while. We have so much to say to each other, we've hardly said anything – anything that matters.

HOLLY (*removing his hand, gently but firmly*). I can't, I'm afraid. I'm meeting somebody in Portsmouth. She's my what they call 'bit on the side', you see, so of course she doesn't like to be kept waiting. And nor do I. (*Smiles.*) But if I'm ever in the old haunts again – good-bye, Lowly. (*Goes out.*)

BROWNLOW (*stroking his hand*). Still real. Still real.

BROWNLOW *goes to the armchair. Sits in it. As he does so, lights up on SMITHERS' drawing room. HOLLY at the piano. Plays Bagatelle as lights go down. Curtain.*